Prisoners in Limbo

Imprisonment for Public Protection

IPP Sentences

©2016 By Michael A O'Brien

Introduction

In 2005 after much outcry from the public and media outlets in relation to serious crime, the government decided to get tough on law and order and brought in the introduction of imprisonment for the public protection to tackle serious crime which included sexual and other violent offences.

However, many more offenders were caught up in this new act and it was called IPP sentences for short. Many onlookers within the criminal justice system saw similarities with life sentenced prisoners who had to show they were no risk to the public before they could be released. IPP sentenced prisoners now had to follow the same criteria before they could even be considered for release. It was down to the parole board to decide if they were a risk of offending or not.

In theory, the only difference between a life sentenced prisoner and one who has been given a IPP sentence is the tariff for a life sentenced prisoner is higher than the tariff given to IPP prisoners by the judge and if for instance they are both granted parole at a later date the IPP prisoners after 10 years can apply to have the licence removed from his file where the life sentenced prisoner cannot do this and remains on parole for the rest of his natural life.

Many prisoners on IPP sentences have had relatively low tariffs some as low as two years however, very few prisoners have actually been released on their actual tariff date and quite a high number of them have done double the recommended tariff sentence set by the judge.

Many families I have spoken to have called IPP sentences a life sentence through the back door and in this book, we will be talking to the families of those who have been affected by these IPP sentences and what it actually means to them and how it affected them.

This book will highlight cases to show how the IPP sentences work, and how unjust this sentence is. One interesting point to note is the fact that many offenders sentenced to IPP have done longer sentences than many sex offenders and paedophiles which the act was originally designed for. Is this an injustice in itself?

This book is dedicated to the memory of the 16 Prisoners who sadly took their own lives whilst serving a IPP sentence god bless them all.

Chapter One - Indeterminate Public Protection Sentence

What is an indeterminate sentence?

Unlike a prisoner with a determinate sentence who must be released at the end of that sentence, those sentenced to life imprisonment or an indeterminate sentence of Imprisonment for Public Protection (IPP) have no automatic right to be released. Instead, such prisoners must serve a minimum period of imprisonment to meet the needs of retribution and deterrence. This punitive period is announced by the trial judge in open court and is known commonly as the "tariff" period.

No indeterminate sentence prisoner can expect to be released before they have served the tariff period in full. However, release on expiry of the tariff period is not automatic. Release will only take place once this period has been served and the parole board is satisfied that the risk of harm the prisoner poses to the public is acceptable. This means that indeterminate sentence prisoners could remain in prison for many more years on preventative grounds after they have served the punitive period of imprisonment set by the trial judge. A release direction can only be made if the parole board is satisfied that the risk of harm the offender poses to the public is acceptable.

The release of indeterminate sentence prisoners is entirely a matter for the parole board.

Imprisonment (or detention) for public protection

An indeterminate sentence of imprisonment (or Detention) for public protection can be imposed in the following circumstances:

Imprisonment for public protection (IPP)

Under Section 225 of the Criminal Justice Act 2003, the courts will impose an indeterminate sentence of IPP when the offender:

- Is aged 18 or over;

- Is convicted of a serious specified violent or sexual offence committed on or after 04 April 2005, for which the maximum penalty is 10 years or more; and who in the court's opinion, poses a significant risk of harm to the public.

The sentence of Imprisonment for Public Protection replaced the automatic life sentence for offences that were committed on or after 04 April 2005.

On 14 July 2008 changes to the above, introduced by Section 47 and Schedule 8 of the Criminal Justice and Immigration Act 2008, come into force. The effect of these changes is that IPP sentences may only be imposed where the offender would be required to serve at least 2 years in custody or (in the cases of offenders under the age of 18) where the offender has a previous conviction for one of a specified list of very serious offences. The act also removes the presumption of risk (requirement for judges to conclude that the offender is dangerous) where there is a previous conviction for violent or sexual crime. It also allows courts greater discretion so that where all the conditions for an IPP sentence are met the court may impose a sentence of IPP, extended sentence or other sentence as it finds most appropriate in the case.

Detention for Public Protection (DPP)

Under Section 226 of the Criminal Justice Act 2003 a sentence of DPP will be imposed in the circumstances above when the offender is under 18 years of age.

Release

All indeterminate sentence prisoners are released on a licence and are supervised by the probation service. The release licence contains several standard conditions that the released prisoner must adhere to. On the recommendation of the parole board the licence may also contain additional conditions that are specific to the individual prisoner such as the requirement to undertake further offending behaviour work in the community or conditions to exclude the individual from certain places in order to protect the victim or victim's family.

Released IPPs:

- Are subject to an IPP licence;

- Can apply to the parole board to have their licence cancelled after 10 years (and if unsuccessful at yearly intervals thereafter);

- May be recalled to prison while the licence remains in force to continue serving their sentence if it is considered necessary to protect the public.

A series of High Court judgments have recently ruled that detention beyond the term of sentence is unlawful, if prisoners sentenced to the IPP are not provided with the appropriate behaviour management courses and assessments in order to present evidence to the parole board as to whether or not they still present a risk. With the prisons facing record overcrowding and a £60m cut in their budgets, and a complete failure on the part of the government to plan for the consequences of the IPP, it is unsurprising that many custodial institutions are unable to provide the courses and assessments needed.

The result is that hundreds of prisoners on IPPs may now be freed if the Court of Appeal upholds the recent judgments. The government is now reviewing the IPP sentence, and this report – particularly the recommendations in this foreword – is intended as a contribution to that review.

The Howard League for penal reform has had concerns over both the principles and practicalities of the IPP since the sentence was first proposed by the former Home Secretary, David Blunkett. Events since the IPP entered the statute book in 2005 have confirmed our worse fears. We believe that the IPP is a misguided sentence that should be abandoned. It is wrong for individuals to be sentenced to indeterminate periods in prison based on acts they might engage in - in the future.

It is also unworkable in the long term. Assessment is an imprecise science that is increasingly measured by the prisoner being able to demonstrate their reduction in risk. With an overcrowded system struggling to provide courses to address offending behaviour, this failure of provision, in turn, drains further resources throughout the secure estate, while adding to the pressure of numbers, as prisoners sentenced to the IPP remain in custody - unable to prove their fitness for release.

A recent parliamentary question covering the period up to April 2007 revealed that in the two years since the IPP was introduced, 2,450 people have been sentenced for public protection. Of these, only five have been released. Because of the length of the sentence and the system's inability to process people, a bureaucratic nightmare is developing - one which will not simply haunt the current government, but also its successors. To add to this, those released on licence under IPP are liable for recall at any time in the following ten years, and annually thereafter if the parole board deems it necessary.

The potential for breach of licence during this long period is immense, and would effectively return anyone who breaches to square one. In other words, the secure estate will see yet more strain placed on its limited resources - not only with incoming IPPs, and those already in the system, but also with those returned to jail after breaching licence conditions. The principle of preventive detention for public protection is one that has been explored before (Rose 2007).

The Prevention of Crime Act 1908 and the Criminal Justice Act 1948 both expanded the use of preventive detention and were eventually repealed after fundamental injustices and withering assessments of their effectiveness. Expanding preventive detention has been tried before and has failed. Repeating historical mistakes is no way to construct a coherent and effective sentencing regime.

Given that the IPP remains on the statute books, however, this report highlights issues that must be addressed to overhaul the current sentence structure. The Howard League for penal reform believes that: Discretion and a fact-sensitive approach to sentencing must be emphasised. The legislation should be amended so that the IPP is used in exceptional circumstances, rather than as a standard prescription.

The Sentencing Guidelines Council should provide guidance on the criteria for exceptional circumstances. Courts should also have discretion to impose a licence of up to ten years, rather than the standard application of ten-year licences, as is currently the case.

To summarise, courts should be given discretion so that where 'there is a significant risk to members of the public of serious harm' the IPP may be imposed, rather than must in relation to the assessment of 'dangerousness', the courts should be provided with a consistent assessment process for all cases where an IPP is considered in order to be meaningful, courts should ensure that the IPP tariff allows sufficient time for an application for parole to be prepared.

Short sentences that do not provide sufficient time indicate that the IPP may not be appropriate in the first place There should be a dedicated officer responsible for those receiving indeterminate sentences in every prison, probation area and youth offending team region. These officers would oversee sentence planning, ensuring that an ongoing risk assessment process is commenced from the beginning of the sentence.

Staff with responsibility for IPPs would have a duty to help these individuals understand the nature of their sentence and to ensure access to offending behaviour programmes and other obligations that must be met. Clearly this has implications for the provision of resources, resources that are currently not there.

Resources must be secured and ring-fenced to ensure that the means on which to base IPP assessment are in place. The Howard League for penal reform is very clear that the resources should not be taken away from other sections of the prison population, for instance lifers, for whom courses and assessments are equally needed and important.

Once again, we return to our initial point – whatever changes are wrought to the IPP sentence, the Howard League for penal reform believes it is essentially unworkable in the long term. Indeterminate Sentences for public protection. Resettlement issues for IPPs should be investigated, with a view to a multi-agency approach to formulating and monitoring a release package that reduces the chances of IPPs reoffending.

Any review should consider how a new release package for all IPPs will work with existing, complex arrangements, such as the prolific and priority offender (PPO) programme and the multi-agency public protection arrangements (MAPPA) for violent and sexual offenders. Crucially, IPP status - and the dangerousness it implies - should automatically engage the assistance of other agencies, such as social services and housing authorities, upon resettlement.

A product of the Criminal Justice Act 2003, the IPP must be imposed upon individuals who are convicted of a serious offence (that is a specified sexual or violent offence carrying a maximum penalty of ten years' imprisonment or more) where 'the court is of the opinion that there is a significant risk to members of the public of serious harm'. the IPP applies to offences that were committed on or after 4 April 2005. There are 153 specified offences eligible for an IPP, compared to just 11 for an automatic life sentence, which the IPP replaced. The offences range from manslaughter and sexual assault, to affray and exposure.

The Court of Appeal has held that courts should presume that anyone convicted of one of these offences who has previous convictions is dangerous, unless this conclusion would be 'unreasonable'.

The IPP is similar to a life sentence in that those sentenced are told by the court that they must serve a minimum prison term ('the tariff'), before being considered for release. All minimum terms are set by the trial judge in open court. Individuals subject to IPPs are released from custody by the Secretary of State at the discretion of the Parole Board, on grounds of public safety.

The offender is then subject to supervision on licence by the probation service for a period of at least ten years, after which time the licence may be terminated by the parole board if it considers it safe to do so. If the licence is not terminated, supervision will continue indefinitely, although further applications can be made to the parole board at yearly intervals.

During licence supervision, those sentenced to IPPs are subject to the same recall arrangements as those on life licences. The decision to recall an IPP licensee to prison is made by the post release section (Public Protection Unit, NOMS), on behalf of the secretary of state, where there is considered to be a risk to public safety.

In 2001, The Halliday Report, Making Punishments Work (Home Office 2001), highlighted a lack of disposals for people who had committed offences which did not carry 'life' imprisonment, but which had a high risk of committing a further offence that would cause serious harm to the public.

In the subsequent Criminal Justice Act 2003, the government thus sought to create a scheme of sentences aimed specifically at offenders who commit sexual and violent offences and who have been assessed as 'dangerous'. The decision to revoke and recall an IPP licensee to prison is made on the recommendation of the parole board, but it can be made without recommendation where the post release section consider there to be an 'immediate and unacceptable' risk to public safety.

The introduction of the IPP heralded a departure from sentencing practices which were determined by the presentation of facts to the court about a specified offence, to decisions based upon the potential future risk that a defendant might pose to the public. In a 2006 appeal judgment, Lord Justice Judge commented on this departure:

'Although punitive in its effect, with far-reaching consequences for the offender on whom it is imposed, it [the IPP] does not represent punishment for past offending...the decision is directed not to the past, but to the future.' A combination of statute and appeal court guidance has led to the IPP sentence being used in almost all instances where offenders have been convicted of the specified offences.

This has resulted in an explosion in numbers of those receiving IPPs in England and Wales. In April 2007, the total adult population in prison serving indeterminate sentences was 8,494. Within this group, the number of prisoners sentenced to an IPP was 2,547.

According to statistics held by NOMS, since April 2005 the use of the IPP has been increasing at the rate of approximately 120 cases per month (accelerating to 160+ in December 2006 and January 2007). In the last quarter of 2006, some 590 prisoners were received into prison on IPPs. This is the equivalent of a prison the size of Altcourse, Brixton or Durham, full of people who are almost certainly in the prison system for a significant period of time.

The increasing frequency with which individuals are being sentenced to indeterminate sentences is having a visible impact on the wider prison population:

To put this in context, within one local prison, our study prison, the forthcoming IMB annual report cites the rate of 'lifers' coming into the prison as increasing by 2% per week, which represents some 10% of all convicted and sentenced prisoners. On a national basis, the situation looks set only to worsen. In a parole board meeting in May 2007, the prison service stated that the population of life sentenced prisoners is projected to be in the region of 25,000 by 2012.

It is likely that this will only serve to exacerbate many of the emerging problems within the criminal justice system today. The use of IPP sentences is no doubt a major contributor towards the current crisis in prison numbers. As of 7 September 2007, there were 80,832 people in prison in England and Wales.

Following the establishment of the Ministry of Justice in May 2007, the issue of prison overcrowding was held to be a central concern, with steps taken to implement early release for non-violent offenders, and plans announced to build 8,000 more prison places by 2012 (Ministry of Justice 2007). However, the policy of expanding prison space, whilst being regressive in the long term, offers no more of a panacea in terms of short-term policy

People serving an Indeterminate Sentence for public protection (IPP) have one of the highest rates of self-harm in the prison system according to a new report published today (23 June) by the Prison Reform Trust.

Figures show that for every 1,000-people serving an IPP there were 550 incidents of self-harm. This compares with 324 incidents for people serving a determinate sentence, and is more than twice the rate for people serving life sentences.

Today over 4,100 people are in prison serving this discredited sentence, unsure when or if they will ever be released. This is despite the abolition of the IPP in 2012, following near universal criticism of the sentence from judges, Parole Board members, HM Prisons Inspectorate, the Prison Governors' Association, staff, prisoners and their families.

The effect of parole board delays, limited resources, poor procedures for managing risk and a lack of available places on offending behaviour programmes means that many IPP prisoners are held for years beyond their original tariff, no longer in prison for what they have done, but for what they might do.

Four out of every five people serving an IPP are still stuck behind bars despite having served their minimum term. 719 people sentenced to an IPP sentence with an original tariff of less than two years are still in custody beyond their tariff. This group would not have been eligible to receive an IPP if they had been convicted of an offence following reforms to the sentence introduced in 2009. Many would have been likely to have received a relatively short determinate sentence.

The impact of ongoing incarceration on the mental health and wellbeing of prisoners and their families is incalculable. Outgoing director of the Prison Reform Trust, Juliet Lyon, together with the shadow prisons minister Jo Stevens MP and Frances Crook, director of the Howard League for Penal Reform, met the families of some of those still held in prison earlier this month, to hear their concerns first hand.

The families expressed their deeply felt frustration, verging on despair. They said that they live in fear of the phone call that tells them that their loved one has lost hope and made an attempt on their own life. These figures released today underline their concerns.

A Court of Appeal ruling earlier this year reaffirmed that it was the responsibility of the government and Parliament to find a solution for those stuck in prison beyond their tariff.

Justice secretary Michael Gove has said, in a recent speech to prison governors, that "there are a significant number of IPP prisoners who are still in jail after having served their full tariff who need to be given hope that they can contribute positively to society in the future." Despite this, the government has ruled out the possibility of introducing new legislation, referring the issue to the parole board.

PRT estimates that the cost so far of incarceration beyond tariff is at least £500 million. Every year the cost of this defunct sentence—that is, the time served over and above what a determinate sentence would have required—is increasing by over £125 million.

Nearly 900 IPP prisoners have yet to reach tariff expiry date. This underlines the urgent need to examine and improve the practices which are taking people so far beyond what the sentencing court envisaged.

Commenting, incoming director of the Prison Reform Trust, Peter Dawson said:

"This report shows the growing toll of despair the IPP sentence is having on prisoners and their families, years after its abolition. Urgent action is needed. The government should convert these discredited sentences into an equivalent determinate sentence, with a clear release date, and provide full support to people returning to their communities. Only then will the damaging legacy of this unjust sentence finally be confined to the history books."

There are still 4,133 people in prison serving an indeterminate sentence for public protection.

When the IPP sentence was originally introduced in 2005, it could be imposed on people who had committed an offence that would have previously attracted a relatively short determinate sentence. As a result, far more were passed by the courts than the original few hundred predicted, placing huge pressure on an already overstretched prison service and Parole Board.

In 2008 reforms were introduced to limit the scope of the IPP, but this runaway sentence continued to be passed by the courts at a considerable rate. Meanwhile, a failure properly to plan and resource the sentence had left thousands of people languishing in jail, some with an original tariff of just a few weeks or so.

In 2008, a Joint report was carried out by HM Chief Inspector of Prisons and the HM Chief Inspector of probation it was called a thematic review of IPP indeterminate sentence for public protection here is what they found with their conclusions.

Key findings and recommendations This report examines the effect of the two new indeterminate sentences – IPP for adults and DPP for children and young people – introduced in the Criminal Justice Act 2003 and available from April 2005. Those sentences were available for a wide range of offences, and average tariffs (the minimum period of detention) were relatively short. The decision was taken initially to manage them as lifers.

This created pressure on the prison, probation and parole systems. 1 The report is based on fieldwork carried out by prison and probation inspectors during the autumn of 2007, at a time when there were around 3,600 IPP prisoners, with an average tariff of 38 months, and 51 DPP prisoners. During 2007, male IPP prisoners had begun to be moved from local prisons to first stage lifer training prisons.

Inspectors collected detailed information on a sample of 30 adult men, six young adult men (18– 21), 12 women and 12 young people (15–18), held in 11 prisons and young offender institutions. They spoke to prisoners and staff, and looked at pre-sentence reports, prison case files and, where possible, at case files in the community.

Key findings Probation Input. Inspectors examined a sample of 48 cases of adult men, young adults and women sentenced to IPPs, to see whether pre-sentence reports (PSRs) properly addressed risk in order to assist the sentencing court. There had been little guidance to probation staff in carrying out this role. Inspectors found:

• Of the 45 cases with pre-sentence reports, fewer than half were informed by a full and accurately completed assessment of current and previous offending behaviour.

• Of those cases, 31 (over two-thirds) had at least one diverse need, such as mental health, substance misuse, ethnicity or learning difficulties.

In only 14 cases did the report demonstrate an understanding of the relevance of the need to the offending or future risk.

• Of the 40 cases which had a risk of harm analysis, only half were judged to have given sufficient consideration to risk issues. Inspectors disagreed with the classification in 17 cases, judging it to be inflated in 16 (40% of cases).

• Overall, the quality of the risk of harm assessment was not sufficient to assist the courts adequately in deciding whether to impose an IPP sentence. 1.5 At the time, IPP prisoners were not within the scope of offender management.

This, and the fact that they were being managed as lifers, limited the engagement of outside probation officers. Inspectors found:

• The supervising probation officer had communicated with the prison or prisoner in just over half of the cases examined.

• This was particularly problematic for the nine prisoners in the sample whose tariffs had expired and who required probation reports. Fewer than half of these reports were informed by an up-to-date OASys (offender assessment), a third lacked a clear assessment of the risks.

The indeterminate sentence for public protection: A thematic review by HM Chief Inspector of Prisons and HM Chief Inspector of probation of harm, just under a half an assessment of the risk of re-offending, and under a quarter a recommendation about release. Only 22% of parole reports were judged sufficient or better.

Adults and young men sentenced to IPP. At the time of the review, prisons were still working to the instruction to treat IPP prisoners as lifers, which involved a complex and bureaucratic system of documents and reports. Inspectors examined the cases of 36 men and spoke to prisoners and the staff responsible for managing them. They found:

• There was a higher than average incidence of prisoners who needed further mental health assessment.

• More than one in five of the prisoners were already over tariff.

• In the local prisons, there were three times as many IPP prisoners as lifers, but there had been no increase in resources. There was no formal strategy for managing IPP prisoners and no ongoing case management. no prisoners had a complete set of documents necessary for risk assessment and sentence management. Apart from basic assessments and preliminary documentation, little else had been done in the average 13 months they had spent in the prison. Staff were struggling to move IPP prisoners to first stage lifer prisons, and were resorting to one-to-one exchanges with other prisons: prioritising them over lifers to avoid them becoming control problems or self-harming. Confusion about the sentence was initially widespread.

Staff had not been specifically trained to understand the sentence and were not in a strong position to assist prisoners ○ most prisoners in the sample were unaware of the life sentence planning process, but were aware they had to complete courses. Identification of targets and availability of offending behaviour programmes was poor, and this led to considerable frustration among prisoners whose release was contingent on completing these programmes.

• In the training prisons there were nearly as many IPP prisoners as lifers in the two adult prisons, and twice as many in the young adult prison, without any increase in resources. Prisons were expecting a one-off payment, but this would not enable them to recruit much-needed staff. IPP prisoners became more frustrated as they realised that courses were not as readily available in training prisons as they had been led to believe: in many cases, the waiting lists were longer than in locals. There was little contact with outside probation staff, or with psychology staff.

Most prisoners had an up-to-date OASys, but one prison was using an inadequate abridged version because of the sudden influx of IPP prisoners. Sentence planning documentation was better than in locals. Nearly all the sample of prisoners had been assessed and knew their targets: in general risk assessment paperwork was of a high standard. Women sentenced to IPP.

There were 77 women serving an IPP at the time of this review, a disproportionately high number for arson offences. They were also managed as lifers, but smaller numbers meant that the pressure was not so great. Inspectors examined the pre-sentence reports, case management and circumstances of 12 women at Styal and New Hall prisons, and spoke to prisoners and the staff responsible for managing them. They found: The indeterminate sentence for public protection:

A thematic review by HM Chief Inspector of Prisons and HM Chief Inspector of Probation that All the 12 women had a pre-sentence report but nearly all were deficient in some respect.

Only five had a full and accurate OASys and only two analyses of risk of harm were of good quality. The level of risk was over-estimated in seven cases.

The pre-sentence reports identified nine of the 12 women as having a mental health need, and eight of these as having additional needs, including learning disability and self-harming behaviour.

Probation had made some contribution to sentence plans and some contact with half the women, but had ongoing engagement with only one.

Four of the women were already over tariff and only three thought they might have done everything they needed to do to be released on tariff. Tariff length was too short for a staged system to work well.

Only two of the women were aware of the life sentence plan process. Seven of the 12 women had an OASys assessment, not all up-to-date, and five had a sentence plan.

The support available to staff was limited and women said that staff lacked knowledge and understanding of the sentence.

This was particularly the case at Styal, which, though it was designated a second stage lifer prison, had held newly-sentenced IPP prisoners for many months after sentence. The average stay there was 18 months, with an average tariff of only 26 months.

New Hall had developed better assessment capacity: formal intelligence testing had revealed that two out of the six women in the sample had learning difficulties.

Children and young people sentenced to DPP 1.8 Young people were managed through the adult lifer system, which ran alongside the training plan system. Neither system was appropriate for supporting long-term planning that included the transition from the under-18 to the young adult estate. Inspectors spoke to 16 young men in three YOIs, as well as the staff who managed them, and examined the pre-sentence reports of 12 and the casework files in the community of six.

They found:

There were deficiencies in the pre-sentence reports prepared by youth offending teams (YOTs). Only five of the 12 had a fully and accurately completed Asset (assessment of risk and need). Offence analysis was incomplete and judgments on potential risk of harm flawed in most cases. Inspectors did not agree with the risk classification in six of the 10 cases which had one: in five it was too high.

Assessments of need identified that around 60% of those sentenced to DPPs had some sort of vulnerability, which might include mental health, conduct disorder or substance misuse.

The quality of casework in YOT files suggested a high degree of involvement with the young person and continuity in case management, though this felt insufficient to the young men themselves.

There was considerable variation between those young people in the two small specialist units (called 'enhanced' units), which are accustomed to holding long and indeterminate sentenced young people, and those held in non-specialist young offender institutions

(YOIs). The specialist units had sufficient trained officers and specialists; the non-specialist sites had fewer trained staff and little support. Around a quarter of young people sentenced to DPP, mainly those under 17, were in the specialist sites.

Those sentenced to DPP were rarely identified on remand, but once sentenced documentation arrived promptly. 8 The indeterminate sentence for public protection: A thematic review by HM Chief Inspector of Prisons and HM Chief Inspector of Probation

Only two-thirds of case files included an Asset, and they were of variable quality. All files contained a training plan, but lifer documentation was incomplete, especially outside the specialist units. Training plans were heavily focused on behaviour and involvement in the regime, rather than the reduction of risk. Even in the two specialist units, practice in relation to target-setting varied. Educational reports were good, and in one case exemplary.

The lack of offending behaviour programmes frustrated young people and staff. There was only one accredited programme, which was not widely available, and no accredited programme for sex offenders.

Staff were not aware of Parole Board members with specialist knowledge of young people, and were concerned that the expectations seemed to be the same as for adults.

Most young people initially thought that their tariff date was their release date. They were generally aware that they had to complete courses to be released. Only half thought they would be able to achieve targets in time for parole. Understanding, and contact with staff and specialists, was better in the specialist sites.

There were problems in continuity of care in the transition from the secure care system to the under-18 prison estate, and also from that estate to young adult prisons. There was little guidance from the YJB to assist this process. Recommendations the Secretary of State should:

• Carry out and publish a costed impact assessment on the effect on the National Offender Management Service of any proposed new criminal sentences.

• Ensure that the parole board has the resources available to be able to carry out parole reviews at the prescribed time for all IPP/DPP prisoners.

• Appoint sufficient specialist parole board members to assess maturity and risk in young people. HMCS should:

• Ensure that court staff provide a clear and understandable written record of the sentencing decision to solicitors and other criminal justice agencies.

• Record the tariff length of IPP prisoners on their IT systems. NOMS should: • Ensure that IPP defendants are identified in advance of sentence so that pre-sentence reports can be subject to quality control arrangements and ○ contain a complete and accurate analysis of risk of serious harm that is capable of assisting the court in determining whether an IPP sentence is the appropriate disposal ○ accurately reflect the diverse needs of offenders being considered for an IPP sentence.

• Clarify who has overall policy responsibility for IPP prisoners and appoint a senior level policy lead.

• Provide sufficient resources to effectively assess, manage, progress and provide reports on the indeterminate-sentenced population within the timescales of their tariffs, including year on year funding.

• Ensure that prison and probation staff working with IPP offenders receive training for their specific roles. The indeterminate sentence for public protection: A thematic review by HM Chief Inspector of Prisons and HM Chief Inspector of Probation 9

• Collate and make publicly available in a single location up-to-date management information about IPP prisoners, including tariff length, ethnicity, location, assessments completed, needs identified, interventions required and progression.

• Complete an intervention needs analysis of those sentenced to IPP and make the resources available to assess and meet these needs in a sufficient number of prisons at appropriate levels of security across the country.

 • Ensure that interventions to reduce risk are adapted to be suitable for those with a learning disability or difficulty.

 • Ensure the seamlessness of sentence planning for IPP offenders, through and beyond custody, by means of the effective implementation of Phase III of the offender management model.

• Ensure that on first arrival IPP prisoners are assessed for their state of mind and provided with appropriate support as required.

• Ensure that self-harm incidents of IPP prisoners are monitored locally by safer custody committees and the information collated centrally.

 • Ensure that IPP prisoners in custody who are primary carers of children (often but not exclusively women) are not moved more than 50 miles away from their families.

• Ensure that the staff managing IPP prisoners in custody and pre-release liaise effectively with multi-agency public protection boards. The YJB should:

• Ensure that pre-sentence reports for those who have committed offences that could attract a DPP sentence, contain a comprehensive analysis of risk of serious harm that includes reference to maturity and vulnerability, to assist the court in deciding how the level of risk can best be managed.

• Routinely collect information about the numbers, risks and needs of young people sentenced to DPP in order to inform a strategic approach to their management.

• Ensure, through effective quality control, that Assets1 are completed to a satisfactory standard to inform individual sentence planning for young people assessed as high risk of harm, and allow aggregated information to be collected about their risks and needs.

• Revise staff guidance to ensure that Assets, pre-sentence reports, vulnerability assessments and all care and management plans require staff to take specific account of young people on remand for offences for which they may receive a DPP sentence.

• Ensure that Asset reviews conducted in youth offending teams are made available to prison staff.

• Develop a strategy to accommodate and manage young people sentenced to DPP within a wider strategy for young people serving long-term sentences.

• Provide guidance for the management of transitions for young people – and the transfer and sharing of information – within the juvenile secure estate and between this and the young adult estate.

• Develop a case management system that will support longer-term sentence planning and transition planning from the juvenile estate to the young adult estate.

• Create a sufficient number of specialist units to accommodate young men serving DPP and other long sentences, resourced to meet their welfare, offending behaviour and learning needs into the young adult estate. 1 Youth Justice Board assessment documentation completed by youth offending teams. 10 The indeterminate sentence for public protection: A thematic review by HM Chief Inspector of Prisons and HM Chief Inspector of Probation

• Develop a range of interventions to meet the complex criminogenic risks and needs of young people committing serious offences.

• Provide specialist training for staff working closely with disturbed adolescents in specialist units, as well as ongoing supervision and support.

• Provide age-appropriate information leaflets about DPP and other indeterminate sentences for young people and their families.

• Liaise with the Probation Service to ensure that those moving from YOT to probation supervision are provided with the resources to maintain the work that has been started over the lifetime of the sentence, including the period on licence.

IPP prisoners: numbers, offences, ethnicity. Largely as a result of the introduction of the IPP sentence, there has been a significant increase in the number of indeterminate-sentenced prisoners, which includes those sentenced to life imprisonment. When the IPP sentence was introduced, there were almost 6,000 lifers in prison. By October 2007, there were over 10,000 indeterminate-sentenced prisoners: 12% of the prison population. They included 6,740 lifers and 3,386 prisoners serving IPP sentences (an annual increase of 111% and rising at a rate of 150 a month). At this point, for the first time, there were more prisoners serving indeterminate sentences than prisoners serving sentences of less than 12 months.

Once the sentence has been decided, the tariff is set in court. It was difficult to obtain information about tariff length as this was not routinely recorded by the courts. Data collected in prison suggested that towards the end of 2007, the average tariff for IPP prisoners was 38 months, with the shortest being 28 days and only 1% over six years.

Nearly 13% were over their minimum tariff period, but only 15 adult IPP prisoners had been released, with two subsequently recalled to prison. At this time, the vast majority (97%) of IPP prisoners were male. Information available indicates that they are younger and have a higher risk of re-offending than the lifer population.

A parole board judge told us that 'IPP prisoners are younger than lifers, have more problems with drugs and alcohol, live chaotic lives and are angry young men who are now stuck in prison getting angrier. Despite the relevant offences being described as violent or sexual, not all would normally be thought of as offences that would attract a life sentence.

At the end of 2007 just over half of IPP prisoners (53%) were convicted of sexual or violent offences; 28% were convicted of robbery; and the rest were convicted of burglary, arson and other offences. The offence profile for women shows that far fewer were convicted of sexual offences and far more of arson, even in circumstances that did not appear to endanger others.

In seven out of 31 cases examined at the pre-sentence stage, PSR authors identified ethnicity as being relevant to the assessment. During our fieldwork, 23% of prisoners interviewed classified themselves as black and minority ethnic, which is in proportion with the ethnic mix of the prison population. However, in none of the establishments visited was the ethnicity of IPP prisoners monitored and figures were not available centrally.

Criminogenic needs and risk of serious harm. The profile of criminogenic needs of IPP prisoners as measured by OASys assessments indicates that they have an average of 6.3 needs from a possible 10, compared to 4.4 for other prisoners

Although criminogenic need is associated with risk of reoffending, it does not necessarily equate to significant risk of serious harm, which is the crucial trigger for an IPP sentence. The OASys assessments used by prisons and probation analyse risk of harm and categorise this risk as low, medium, high or very high. In the legislation, what constitutes a 'significant risk' is not defined, though 'serious harm' is defined as 'death or serious personal injury, whether physical or psychological'.

There is not a direct read-across between OASys and the provisions of the Act. However, guidance issued to practitioners in June 2005 states that there is 'a measure of compatibility' between 'significant risk of serious harm' and the OASys category of 'high andvery high risk of serious harm'. Sentencing guidelines issued in September 2007 confirmed that the definitions of serious harm in the Act and OASys are comparable.

The risk profile of IPP prisoners varies considerably. OASys assessments of risk of harm place 68% of IPP prisoners in the high-risk category but only 6% in the very high risk of harm category, while a quarter are assessed as low or medium risk. Part of the explanation for these variations is the presumption that the threshold of significant risk of serious harm has been reached if the offender has committed any specified offence even a less serious one in the past.

In this context, pre-sentence reports are crucial in providing a clear and accurate analysis of the risk of serious harm to assist the court in deciding whether this presumption is unreasonable in the particular case. we identified concerns about the reliability and consistency of the risk assessment process.

Mental health OASys assessments suggest that IPP prisoners have more mental health problems than other prisoners. The graph below indicates that higher proportions of IPP prisoners have needs in a range of areas associated with mental health.

Self-harm, OASys assessments identify that both IPP prisoners and lifers have a raised risk of self-harm and suicide (37%) compared to other prisoners (23%). Data from the Prison Service's Safer Custody Group also confirm that IPP prisoners have a raised incidence of self-harm.

This is consistent with their complex needs, the uncertainty about length of detention and their frustrations in making progress this shows that the number of self-harm incidents among IPP prisoners since the sentence was introduced has risen more steeply than their proportion in the prison population.

Most of those receiving an IPP sentence would, in any case, have been given a significant custodial sentence. However, the response of NOMS when the sentence was introduced to manage them as lifers it assigned them to a different, and much more rigid and bureaucratic system of assessment and allocation. Moreover, the need for them to show that they had addressed risk by the end of the tariff period placed a considerable burden on the capacity of that system, in the context of shorter and occasionally very short tariffs.

The lifer management system requires newly convicted indeterminate-sentenced prisoners to spend up to five months in a local prison where pre-sentence documentation is collated, initial needs assessed and an allocation decision made. They are then transferred to a first stage lifer (training) prison for more in-depth assessment to identify risk factors, complete sentence plans and begin interventions to reduce risk.

Reviews take place at least annually and at some stage the lifer moves to a second stage lifer prison where intervention work is completed. Once tariff has expired and it is deemed appropriate by the parole board and endorsed by the Secretary of State, the lifer usually moves to a third stage open or resettlement prison to be prepared for release back into the community. Only a limited number of prisons are designated as lifer prisons at different stages. By the time IPP prisoners entered the lifer system, there had also been significant changes in the national management arrangement for such prisoners.

There had been a national prison service body, the lifer Unit, with responsibility for managing the progress of lifers, and for overseeing their review and recall. In December 2003 responsibility for lifer review and recall moved from the Prison Service to the Home Office and soon after, the management of lifers within the prison system was devolved to Prison Service area managers. By December 2004 lifer review and recall had been rebadged as part of the National Offender Management Service (NOMS), and at the same time had experienced an 18% drop in staffing – just as its case load was burgeoning to IPP population and self-harm incidents % 16 14 12 10 8 6 4 2 0 2005 2006 2007 2008 Year IPP % of population (Jul 07) IPP % self-harm incidents.

The indeterminate sentence for public protection: A thematic review by HM Chief Inspector of Prisons and HM Chief Inspector of Probation twice its previous size. The Prison Service and individual prisons continued to manage IPP prisoners as lifers as best they could, although responsibility for this decision and its consequences lay with NOMS. A senior official told us 'lifer work is at the edge of the universe for senior policy people.

They are only interested when something goes wrong. The aim, within the NOMS model, was for end-to-end offender management of each individual prisoner during and beyond custody. High risk and persistent and prolific offenders were the first prisoners to be managed under this model, for obvious reasons. That definition includes many of those sentenced to IPPs. However, because they were classified as lifers, IPP prisoners did not come within the offender management model until phase III, scheduled for the beginning of 2008. As a result, they were not subject to the same level of offender management as those serving determinate sentences.

The Youth Justice Board (YJB) did not issue guidance to secure establishments on the management of children and young people serving DPP sentences in the juvenile estate. Nor did the Prison Service's Women and Young People's Group (W&YPG) issue guidance specifically on the management of the IPP sentence for women, and no additional resources were provided. Although there have been fewer juveniles sentenced to DPP or women sentenced to IPP than adult men, the lack of strategy or guidance left Youth Offending Teams, juvenile establishments and women's prisons to develop their own systems.

 For children and young people, these were based on practice with other indeterminate-sentenced young people and for women, on current practice with women lifers. Regional briefings for probation staff before the Act was implemented focused on the new sentencing framework and the introduction of the community order. In June 2005, after the Act was implemented, NOMS issued a national guide7 which made extensive reference to the preparation of pre-sentence reports, as well as including risk management plans. However, this was not supported by sufficient specific training. Few probation areas that we visited appeared to have considered, even in the broadest terms, the significant resource implications of the new sentence and how these could be managed.

We found no evidence of areas identifying potential IPP cases before trial to ensure that pre-sentence reports properly addressed the difficult concept of identifying significant risk of serious harm, to meet the definition of dangerousness. The consequences were evidenced in our examination of pre-sentence reports.

Local prisons are not resourced to carry out anything more than basic work with a small number of potential and newly convicted life-sentenced prisoners. However, some had received over 100 IPP prisoners, with the instruction to treat them as lifers, and it proved extremely difficult to move adult male prisoners on to their usual first stage lifer prison. In July 2007, there were more than 2,500 such prisoners in local prisons, some of whom had been there for over two years.

Many were not assessed and did not have a sentence plan. They did not have a clear idea of what they needed to do to progress and the locals did not offer the range and type of offending behaviour courses they needed. Those who did progress to first stage centres in training prisons, which in theory were better resourced and equipped to deal with them, found these prisons could not cope with the numbers involved either. A large influx of IPP prisoners from locals in early 2007 caused significant bottlenecks.

Little assessment work or intervention had been done before their arrival and many were close to tariff expiry. Promised additional resources did not materialise and the lack of prior 7 National Guide to the Criminal Justice Act 2003 sentences for public protection. Edited version 1, June 2005. The indeterminate sentence for public protection: A thematic review by HM Chief Inspector of Prisons and HM Chief Inspector of Probation 17 assessment meant prisoners were often in the wrong prison to access the interventions they required.

It also became evident that the parole system was under-resourced for the increased number of oral hearings required for indeterminate prisoners and recalled prisoners.

Parole dossiers were often late because prisons lacked capacity to prepare them. The parole board annual report for 2006/7 reported that only 38% of parole reports were received on time, and that at one point during the year a third of oral hearings were being deferred. They also predicted a staggering 4,000 oral hearings a year for lifer and IPP cases by 2009.

A judicial review on behalf of two IPP prisoners whose tariffs had expired or were approaching expiry found that the Secretary of State had acted unlawfully in failing to provide for such prisoners to be able to address risk before tariff expiry, and also that it followed that once tariff had expired, they were held unlawfully.

The government appeal against this judgment was dismissed, though the Court of Appeal did not uphold the finding that post-tariff detention was unlawful.

The court nevertheless reasserted that the secretary of state had acted unlawfully and that 'there has been a systemic failure on the part of the secretary of state to put in place the resources necessary to implement the scheme of rehabilitation necessary to enable the relevant provisions of the 2003 Act to function as intended' and that if the situation continued, detention could indeed become unlawful.

An internal policy review recommended that phase III of the implementation of offender management in January 2008 should bring IPP prisoners (and young people sentenced to DPP aged 18 and over) into scope, and that they should be managed as determinate-sentenced prisoners rather than lifers. Instructions were issued that newly-sentenced IPP prisoners and those with an up-to-date OASys should be prioritised by tariff, with the gradual assimilation of the remaining prisoners over subsequent months.

With OASys replacing lifer sentence planning, paper and reporting processes were simplified.

However, with no significant increase in resources, the prioritisation of the ever-growing IPP population will inevitably detract from the attention paid to other prisoners, not least lifers.

Changes have also been made to the legislation, limiting the availability of IPP/DPP sentences to those with a minimum tariff of over two years. This should reduce the numbers sentenced to an IPP by up to an estimated 30%. However, those sentenced previously with a tariff of two years or less remain in prison subject to an indeterminate sentence, where they are likely to stay well beyond tariff. Although the NOMS guide, issued in June 2005, identified the criteria for eligibility for potential IPP/DPP prisoners, it did not offer any guidance about how probation staff should engage with IPP prisoners before their release, or explicitly address their status as lifers.

This omission was only remedied by the revisions to the lifer manual that were circulated to probation areas in June 2006 but were not widely publicised and may well have gone unnoticed. A national guide to working with high risk prisoners also made some reference to IPP prisoners but did not address their particular needs in any detail.

At the time of this review, IPP prisoners had made relatively little impact on probation areas. Few had been released and, due to their exclusion from phase II of the offender management model, little systematic pre-release work was being carried out. With little engagement at the initial stages, this was likely to make their future extended supervision problematic.

Moreover, the risk and needs profile of these prisoners suggests that they are likely to make significant demands on probation resources as phase III of the offender management model is rolled out, and during extended, even lifetime, periods of licence in the community.

IPP sentences are based on assumptions about an individual's potential for future serious offending). Thorough assessment of the likelihood and potential impact of re-offending in pre-sentence reports (PSRs) is therefore crucial.

These reports are informed, for adults, by an OASys assessment that contains an assessment of general criminogenic need, or likelihood of reoffending, and a more detailed risk of harm assessment.

The risk of harm assessment makes further discriminations about who is at risk of harm from the offender, in what circumstances and with what degree of imminence, and comes to a conclusion about the level of risk of harm posed by the offender.

In our sample of 48 IPP prisoners, only three had no PSR, but a further five had no OASys completed. Of the 40 cases with an OASys, only 22 had been completed fully or accurately, 11 so overall less than half of the whole sample (46%) had a PSR informed by a full and accurately completed assessment of current and previous offending behaviour. 3.4 of the 45 adult IPP cases with a PSR, 31, or over two-thirds, had a special need identified, with some having more than one such need. These included mental health in 21 cases, ethnicity in seven, substance misuse in six, learning difficulties in one, age in another and social care history in another.

But in only 14 (one female and 13 male) of the 31 cases had the PSR author demonstrated an understanding of how the need was relevant to the offending and to future risk. 3.5 An analysis of reoffending, risk of harm screening, and a full risk of harm analysis were undertaken in all 40 cases where an OASys assessment had been completed.

Although the risk of harm screenings was considered accurate in 88% of cases, only 58% of the full risk of harm analyses were judged to have given sufficient consideration to the relevant risk issues. We disagreed with the classification in 17 cases, judging it to be inflated in 16. 3.6 Less than half of the 45 PSRs clearly stated who was at risk from the offender and only 22% separated out the likelihood of harm and the impact of that harm.

The pattern of offending was documented in 33 (73%) of the 45 reports examined, but an analysis of the offence was present in only

22 (49%). 3.7 Overall, the quality of the PSRs and the OASys assessments completed for the IPP cases were not sufficient to assist the courts adequately in establishing whether to impose an IPP sentence, or whether the presumption that one should be imposed could be rebutted.

Risk of harm assessments were deficient in a substantial number of cases, and inaccurate classifications meant that the court was not properly advised as to whether some offenders reached the threshold of dangerousness. In our opinion, if such an exercise had been carried out, presentence reports could have advised that the risks posed in <u>19 of the 48 cases could have been managed by a different sentence</u>.

Probation case management. At the time of the fieldwork, IPP prisoners were not within the scope of offender management, which meant there was no specific requirement for probation officers in the community to communicate routinely with the prison holding them. They were treated as lifers, and probation involvement with lifers was traditionally predicated on a working relationship being established with the prisoner over a lengthy period in custody, focusing on safe preparation for release.

This model clearly did not work for the IPP population. Probation involvement was therefore limited and not generally sufficient to meet needs. 3.9 Just over half the 35 case files examined, of both men and women, indicated that the supervising probation officer had communicated with the relevant custodial staff during the custodial phase and with the prisoner, mainly in writing. In 64% of cases where the prisoner had spent more than 12 months in custody, probation staff had contributed to the reviews of OASys.

Eight of the 35 case files suggested probation involvement in sentence planning, and four showed evidence of the supervising probation officer's contribution to the ongoing assessment of the prisoner's risk of harm to others. In only three instances had there been a meeting between the supervising probation officer, the prisoner and a member of prison staff, including one where this had involved a discussion about a transfer to a training prison.

There was evidence of substantial numbers of internal transfers of IPP cases between probation staff during the period of the sentence.

Fifteen of the 35 prisoners had been held by two different probation officers during the first year of sentence and one by three different probation officers. Several prisoners in their second year of sentence had also had changes of probation officer, including one who had had two different probation officers in the first year and a further three in the second year.

However, with the outside probation officer so peripheral to case management, this had less serious consequences than if these offenders had been in the scope of offender management arrangements.

The picture was more problematic with regard to parole reports for the nine prisoners whose tariffs had expired. Here, the consequences of probation's lack of ongoing involvement during sentence became evident. In only four of the nine cases was there clear evidence that the probation parole report had been informed by an up-to-date OASys.

Six included a clear assessment of risk of harm, five an assessment of the likelihood of re-offending and seven a recommendation about release, but only one included a comprehensive risk management plan. In only 62% of relevant cases had the victim or their family been offered contact with the probation service, although there was clear evidence that the victim liaison officer had provided relevant information about the victims' views on the proposed release conditions.

There was some evidence in case files of active engagement with multi-agency public protection arrangement (MAPPA) processes, but the overall quality of the reports was disappointing, with only two of the nine (22%) judged sufficient or better.

At the time of this review, prisons were still working under the instruction to treat IPP prisoners as lifers. This involved a complex and bureaucratic set of paperwork, with 28 separate forms plus reports to be completed as the prisoner moved through the various stages of the lifer process.

The day-to-day management of this complex paper system was demanding. The decision to treat IPP prisoners as lifers also meant that when they were finally moved from a local to one of the relatively few training prisons specialising in indeterminate sentenced prisoners, they were often located long distances from their home area. We looked in depth at the cases of 36 men, half of whom were in Birmingham, Nottingham and Wandsworth local prisons and half in Aylesbury (where we examined a sample of six young adults), Garth and Parkhurst training prisons. The average stay of those we interviewed in local prisons was 13 months, ranging from one to 27 months.

This compared to nine months in training prisons, with a range of between two and 18 months, reflecting the delays in moving IPP prisoners from locals into the training estate.

During fieldwork, 23 of the 36 young adults and adult IPP prisoners in our sample completed a GHQ-12, a measure of psychological wellbeing. A score of four or greater on this questionnaire would normally, in a community setting, trigger further mental health assessment. Fourteen (61%) met or exceeded this threshold. This compares with 52% of men and 27% of young adults screened at a known high risk time within a month of entry to custody as part of our mental health thematic last year. It suggests that our sample of IPP prisoners was a troubled group. However, only in Aylesbury was there any formal involvement of mental health in-reach teams with IPP prisoners, and this was for limited cases.

This is not to say that individual IPP prisoners might not have been picked up on reception if they had had previous mental health input or were on psychotropic medication on arrival, but if this was the case there was little sharing of this information with prison staff. Local prisons. At Birmingham, Nottingham and Wandsworth, IPP prisoners made up three quarters of the total indeterminate-sentenced population (lifers and IPPs), which averaged about a hundred in each prison. Resources had not increased in line with the numbers and none of the prisons had a fulltime lifer manager, although all had full-time clerks and another lifer-trained staff who contributed the equivalent of about a full-time officer. There was no ongoing case management for any of the IPP prisoners and none of the three locals had a formal strategy for managing them.

The 18 files they examined all had the pre-first stage paperwork completed together with an initial allocation report. The local prisons were aiming to do the basics that they usually did for lifers: conducting a multi-agency lifer risk assessment panel (MALRAP) and completing the pre-stage one documentation. Some lifer governors did not seem to be aware that OASys might be available from outside probation.

PSRs were present in only four of the 18 prison files, even though we knew these had been completed in most cases, and only one file contained a probation post sentence report. Two contained a multi-agency lifer review panel report (MALRAP), which is part of the inter-agency information exchange that takes place for lifers soon after sentence, and 11 contained an OASys completed in prison. There was no input from psychologists to the assessment process and scarce seconded probation resources. Little else had been done in the average 13 months the men had been in prison.

All three locals cited the difficulty of moving IPP prisoners on to a first stage lifer prison as the major barrier to progression. At one, IPP prisoners were typically waiting 18 months for their first move. There were not enough places and local managers resorted to making direct contact with prisons, sometimes out of area, to negotiate individual moves.

IPP prisoners were being prioritised for moves to stage one centres when these came up, causing a consequent problem for mandatory lifers.

When first introduced, the IPP sentence was confusing for many criminal justice professionals. In fieldwork, we found examples where judges' sentencing comments were unclear about the status of the sentence and, in a few cases, this had resulted in IPP prisoners being treated for several months as if they had a determinate sentence.

Many prisoners also reported that they were confused, having received contradictory information from different criminal justice staff involved in their case, often relying on their solicitors or other prisoners for information. Only two of the 18 prisoners in our local prison sample reported receiving any information at the time of sentencing and both said this was inadequate. Only seven of the 60 probation case files examined contained evidence that the implications of an IPP sentence had been discussed with the prisoner at the time of sentence.

Fifteen of the 18 reported that they had subsequently received information from a lifer officer in prison, generally in the form of a lifer booklet and verbal explanation, but most again reported that this was inadequate. We were told that the timing of this initial contact was variable, ranging from several days to several months after sentence. Only seven of the 18 reported ever seeing the lifer manager. Even for those who were seen by staff in the early days, there was still confusion around the sentence. Some positive comments were made about their contact with lifer staff.

A number of the prisoners reported to us that their needs during the first days after sentence had not been met. Some had been held on their first night with short-term determinate prisoners and it was common for them to share cells with very short-term remand or convicted prisoners. They said this was unsettling, especially when their cellmate was released, which happened frequently.

Most ongoing contact with staff in local prisons was with personal officers, but this did not necessarily help with their sentence as many were not lifer trained. Contact with external probation staff was described as poor and infrequent, with the majority of those interviewed saying they had been contacted only once.

Bearing in mind that IPP prisoners were not in scope of offender management arrangements, brief post-sentence contact was all that would be expected. From the probation case files, it was clear that just over half of the IPP prisoners had met or communicated with their probation officer after sentence to discuss the IPP sentence with them, mostly by letter.

Only four of the 18 prisoners reported contact with other prison specialists, such as psychology, and two with mental health professionals. Contact had increased for those who were nearing their parole date

Eleven of the 18 prisoners in local prisons were unaware of the life sentence planning process. Only four reported having an OASys assessment, although case files indicated that 11 had an up to-date report, with all but one of the men at Nottingham and Birmingham having an OASys. Only three reported having a sentence plan and there was little evidence of these in case files. When asked about what targets they were working towards, prisoners in locals said very few had been set by staff. Prisoners saw their time in these prisons as wasted, with little or no progress made. However, some had taken their own action to get on courses despite not having completed assessments or knowing what their formal targets were.

With greater knowledge about the sentence, prisoners were more frustrated about their lack of progress in moving through the system and more aware of the consequences for them.

Across all three locals, identification of targets and availability of relevant offending behaviour programmes (OBPs) was poor. Prisoners were trying to access whatever courses were available despite not knowing what their targets were. They said this helped them to feel a sense of purpose and progression while waiting for transfer.

Training prisons. The three training prisons visited, Aylesbury (young adults), Garth and Parkhurst, had the advantage of a larger accumulation of paperwork from the court and from local prisons. For our sample of 18 prisoners, confidential summary dossiers had usually arrived, although all prisons claimed this was a slow process and the information they contained was often incomplete. Any vulnerability to self-harm was usually noted, as was some description of the background offending from probation in the form of a PSR (seven cases) and/or a post-sentence report (eight cases) and or a MALRAP (four cases).

All the cases seemed to have drawn from an OASys assessment, although it was not clear whether this was from probation or had been completed in prison. Aylesbury benefited from paperwork from Feltham, which was completed to a high standard.

Garth was struggling to cope with an influx of 115 IPP prisoners from locals at the beginning of 2007, many of whom had arrived with little information. The 12 files examined at Parkhurst and Aylesbury showed more evidence of progress, with half fully assessed, including two cases in which there were in-depth psychological assessments and two with progress reports on interventions completed. Four to six cases contained evidence of second stage work, with sentence planning boards held and progress reviews submitted.

On the whole, both the OASys and lifer sentence plans (LSPs) were detailed and analytical. Parkhurst staff pointed out that many of their IPP prisoners were convicted of domestic violence. The only interventions for this were the cognitive self-change programme, for which they had only four vacancies, and healthy relationships, which had a long waiting list. This was one of many examples where a large number of IPP prisoners were chasing a small number of programme places.

At the adult trainers, Garth and Parkhurst, IPP prisoners made up between a third and a half of the total population of indeterminate-sentenced prisoners (lifers and IPPs), which was over 300 in each case. In Aylesbury YOI, IPP prisoners accounted for two-thirds of the indeterminate sentenced population, reflecting the national trend for them to be younger than lifers.

None of the prisons had received any increase in resources, although they had been told this would be forthcoming in the form of a one-off payment.

This would prevent the money being used to recruit staff, which incurred a year-on-year cost and was where the greatest need lay. Staff in all three establishments said they had received little or no support from Prison Service headquarters or NOMS.

In our sample of 60 IPP prisoners, 12 were women with an average age of 34 years. They were located in two prisons – New Hall, a first stage lifer centre, and Styal, a second stage lifer centre which we selected as they held the greatest number of women IPP prisoners. When we selected our sample, 77 women were serving IPP sentences.

Far fewer women than men had attracted this sentence and the pressures on the lifer system in female establishments were correspondingly less. The profile of IPP offences indicates that far fewer women than men had been sentenced to IPP for sexual offences and far more for arson. Of those interviewed, six had committed violent offences against the person, four arson and criminal damage, one robbery and one a sexual offence. Pre-sentence reports to court. All 12 women had a PSR prepared for the court. Seven of these were clearly based on an OASys, but only five of the OASys documents were completed fully and accurately and contained enough detail to assist with the PSR. Nine of the 12 women were identified with a mental health need.

In our recent mental health, thematic we found that 27% of women reported previous mental health treatment in the community, which suggests that the prevalence of mental health need in women IPP prisoners may be disproportionately high. Eight of these had additional needs, including learning difficulty, alcohol dependency, ethnicity and self-harming behaviour.

The implications of this are significant for the capacity of women to cooperate with their sentence plan and make progress, especially when taken together with other jeopardies such as mental health problems and possible drug or alcohol misuse.

Less than half of the women (five of 12) had an OASys completed fully and accurately at the presentence stage, and only two of the analyses of risk of harm within OASys came to an accurate conclusion about the level of risk posed by the individual woman. In seven cases, the level of risk was over-estimated. In only two reports did the PSR author make a clear recommendation for an IPP sentence. For most other cases, a custodial sentence was acknowledged as inevitable, but no type was specified. In one case, a community order had been recommended.

From our analysis, pre-sentence reports could have advised that the risks posed by six of the 12 women could have been managed in a different way than by an IPP sentence. Probation case management 5

There was evidence of a contribution to sentence planning in only half of the six case files reviewed in the community. In only one was it evident that probation had met with prison staff and the prisoner post-sentence and in none had they contributed to decisions about movement to another prison.

Probation staff had communicated with half of the women post-sentence and, like male prisoners, this was usually in writing. Two of the women had parole reports completed by probation, but both had limited or missing risk management plans. The experience of women in prisons. Some women reported particular problems when returning to prison after being sentenced, with little specific support offered at a time when they felt shocked and extremely vulnerable.

The women reported that contact with lifer officers was more frequent and consistent at New Hall than at Styal. Seven of the 12 women (five at New Hall and two at Styal) said they had had contact with the lifer manager. In both prisons, women said staff lacked knowledge and understanding of the IPP sentence, making it difficult to get clear information about what they needed to do to progress.

Much of the information provided was designed for lifers rather than IPP prisoners. Women at Styal said they gathered much of their information from other women in the prison. Only two of the 12 were aware of the life sentence plan process and at what stage they were.

Those interviewed reported minimal contact with any specialist or probation staff. Seven of the 12 women had an OASys assessment, although not all of these were up to date, and only two said they really understood the document and their risk factors.

Five had a sentence plan, but seven said they were aware of targets and courses they needed to achieve and attend. Three were on OBPs and six had previously completed some type of intervention, although four of these six were unclear whether these were relevant to their risk factors. Women at Styal were required to refer themselves to courses.

Only three of the 12 women thought they had done everything required to be released on tariff expiry and four were already over tariff. The majority of women knew they would not be released if they had not achieved all their targets, but had limited knowledge of the further implications this might have for them.

As with men, very little planning had gone into how women IPP prisoners would be managed. Styal was formally designated as a stage two lifer centre for women, but had held on remand a number of IPP prisoners with multiple and complex needs. Once sentenced it was the expectation that they would transfer to a stage one lifer centre, for completion of the initial lifer sentence planning documentation. However, the women in our sample had waited an average of 18 months in Styal (ranging from seven to 27 months) for a move to a stage one lifer centre, when their average tariff was 26 months, and they needed to be able to demonstrate progress by tariff expiry.

Staff at Styal told inspectors they could hold a maximum of 12 IPP prisoners, and had eight at the time of the review. Although it was a designated second stage lifer prison where women were expected to address their offending behaviour, it offered only specialist thinking skills (ETS) and a short duration drug programme to which the women were expected to self-refer.

In contrast, New Hall had operated as a first stage centre since July 2006 and was developing its capacity to assess lifers on arrival, although it was still under complement for psychologists. Several of the IPP prisoners in our sample had been transferred to New Hall when it came on stream, but in the meantime, some had self-referred and completed programmes at Styal before their needs had been assessed.

Expecting to be released at tariff expiry was not really based on anything other than hope. I have no sentence plan completed... told I'm a 'model prisoner' and got on with things. Have a trusted position in prison so would like to think the parole board would recognise this and release me. Not having a release date is very frightening. Leaves me hanging on a thread. Not a clue what I have to do. Done seven months and just been left… gets me upset. Don't think I will get home. Women IPP prisoners Case Study K received a tariff of one year, 206 days that had already expired. She completed specialist thinking skills on remand having referred herself after her pre-sentence OASys assessment.

Despite this OASys not being available to prison staff, K was fully aware of her risk factors and also self-referred to the counselling, assessment, referral, advice and through care drugs service. The lifer documentation completed betrayed the lack of lifer experience among staff. Her lifer profile, which should record the results of specialist assessment, was completed as an interview. Under 'any further assessments required?' the response recorded was 'K states not at this time'. She was subsequently transferred to another prison for lifer assessment, but at this point was already past her parole date and had addressed the risk factors identified in the pre-sentence OASys.

The indeterminate sentence for public protection: A thematic review by HM Chief Inspector of Prisons and HM Chief Inspector of Probation 35 5.18 Here the psychology department had a reciprocal arrangement with clinical psychologists in training who carried out formal intelligence testing (WAIS III) with the women.

They had identified low IQ levels in the borderline range and below among several of the women convicted of arson, including two of our small sample of six women. This had been discovered serendipitously as IQ screening is not a normal part of the assessment carried out at stage one lifer centres. The implications of this are significant for the capacity of women to make progress, especially when taken together with other jeopardies such as mental health problems and drug or alcohol misuse.

During fieldwork, all 12 of the women IPP prisoners in our sample completed a GHQ-12, a measure of psychological wellbeing. A score of four or greater on this questionnaire would normally, in a community setting, trigger further mental health assessment. Seven (58%) met or exceeded this threshold. This compares with 65% of women, screened at a known high risk time within a month of entry to custody, as part of our mental health thematic last year. However, there was little formal involvement of mental health in-reach teams with IPP assessment, though staff at Styal reported that two women had severe mental health difficulties and it was very difficult to get them to cooperate with their sentence plan.

They told us that they were trying to arrange a transfer to the Primrose unit for dangerous and severe personality disorder at Low Newton prison for one, and to an NHS secure unit for the other. 5.20 Some of the women had resisted transferring to New Hall from Styal. Once they were settled into Styal, it felt like a reverse move to a first stage lifer prison. One woman was the primary carer of her children who lived close to the prison and she was reluctant to move away from them. It was also known that New Hall did not offer any more OBPs, so the women did not believe they would be any better off there.

The reality was that tariff length was too short for a staged system to work, especially where resources could not be deployed promptly. Staff felt they were supported in managing IPP prisoners by being able to discuss their needs at quarterly meetings with the Women and Young People's Group (W&YPG) at Prison Service headquarters and with a named NOMS coordinator. However, neither of these parts of the organisation had any operational responsibility for these prisons

In 2010, the Prison Reform Trust and the Institute for Criminal Policy Research also published a joint report. The report, said that the ill-drafted indeterminate sentence for public protection IPP had wrought havoc in the justice system and should be reviewed by the government as a matter of some urgency.

A prisoner also wrote to NOMS (National Offenders Management Service) asking for statistics on Ipp prisoners which was published in inside times the prisoner's newspaper it makes grim reading but will give you an insight on how difficult it is to get parole once you have been given an IPP sentence.

This is what this IPP prisoner had to say:

I contacted NOMS in order to obtain statistics relating to IPP prisoners, which I think your readers will find interesting. The following figures are as of the 17th of November 2010, the last date from which figures are available.

*The total IPP population – 6,380
*The number of IPPs held in open conditions – 260
*The number of IPPs who have been released – 190 (this figure includes those released and subsequently recalled but does not include those who have been deported)
*The number of male adult IPPs in prison whose offence was sexual – 1,594

The number of male adult IPPs whose index offence was sexual who have been released – 21 I also asked for the number of male adult sex offender IPPs who are currently held in open conditions but this figure could not be supplied because the total figure amounts to 5 people or fewer and could potentially lead to the identification of individuals.

IPPs are mainly violent or sexual offenders, but from the above figures we can see the dramatic differences between the violent and the sexual offenders in the release rates and number of each in open conditions. Some people may be surprised that only 21 IPP sex offenders have been released in the 6 years that IPP has been in force.

The recent Green Paper on Sentencing & Rehabilitation gave the impression that the government might be thinking about abolishing the IPP sentence or at least making retrospective changes, but when it was published there was no mention of abolishing IPPs. It seems that the MoJ decided that the easiest solution to the IPP problem is to keep IPPs locked up, because there are cuts to the Probation Service and they barely coping now with people on license, let alone if a couple of thousand IPPs were to be released.

Many IPPs will be required to live in approved premises (hostels) when released and there are not enough spaces available now. So, warehousing' IPPs must seem to be the easiest option to the MoJ. I am an IPP with a 2-year tariff but I have now served 5 years, I have played the game, obeyed all the rules and been a model prisoner, but, despite 2 oral hearings my chances of progressing to open conditions or being released are still zero.

I am stable, mentally strong and I can cope well so I realise that I must now put all thoughts of progression or release out of my mind and try to make a life for myself in prison. I can only hope that one day the government will come to its senses and abolish the IPP, and make it retrospective. But I fear this is a forlorn hope.

The IPP was eventually abolished in 2012 by the Legal Aid, Sentencing and Punishment of Offenders Act.

Two Investigative Journalists for vice news Maeve McClenaghan and Ben Bryant investigated the problems with IPP after IPP sentences were abolished here is what they found:

Thousands of prisoners — many of who committed relatively minor crimes — are stuck in British jails on an obsolete life sentence at an annual cost to the UK taxpayer of more than 119 million pounds ($180 million), a VICE News investigation has found.

Indeterminate Sentences for Public Protection (IPP) were introduced 10 years ago to keep criminals behind bars until they were no longer deemed a risk to the public, but where their crimes did not warrant a fixed life sentence.

They were scrapped in 2012 after Justice Secretary Kenneth Clarke admitted they were "unclear, inconsistent and have been used far more than ever intended" — but nothing was done to address the thousands already in prison on a seemingly never-ending sentence. In an exclusive investigation, VICE News has uncovered the legacy of the IPP sentence. We spoke to prisoners, former prisoners, family members, lawyers, and a former judge, analysed government data and prison inspection reports, and issued a raft of Freedom of Information (FOI) requests. We found:

- There are 4,612 IPP prisoners remaining in jail three years after the sentences were abolished and not a single one has a set release date.
- Although they were designed for the most dangerous offenders, IPP sentences were given out for relatively minor crimes including affray (fighting in public), minor criminal damage worth less than 20 pounds, and shoplifting.
- Rehabilitation courses prisoners must complete to be released are frequently unavailable.
- Sixteen IPP prisoners have killed themselves since the sentence was abolished and inmates sentenced to IPPs have a higher suicide rate overall.
- Once released from jail, IPP prisoners can spend their life on probation. Since 2012, more than 50 percent of those released have already been recalled.
- Each year it costs the government at least 119 million pounds to house IPP prisoners who have completed their mandatory minimum sentence.

Now, a retired judge and 10-year veteran of the UK's parole board has called on the justice secretary to release IPP inmates who have served their recommended term.

After seven years in practice, the controversial sentences were abolished in 2012 after the European Court of Human Rights ruled that prisoners had the right to know how long they were being held for. UK courts stopped handing out the sentences, but the ban did nothing to impact those already serving an IPP.

Trapped in the System

VICE News found that, three years after the sentences were abolished, more than three quarters of the 4,612 IPP prisoners still stuck in the system have passed the minimum term set by the

court. More than 200 have been in prison for nearly a decade —
despite being given a minimum sentence of less than two years.
IPP sentences were introduced to deal with serious and prolific
offenders. The original legislation meant that they applied to 153
specified offenses, but our investigation found that they were
handed out far more widely than ever intended.

The few hundred sentences that were expected snowballed into
judges handing down 8,701 IPP sentences in just seven years —
some for crimes far less serious than those specified in the original
legislation.

We also found that these extreme sentences were issued for
offenses as minor as affray and shoplifting. As many as 225
people received one for assault occasioning actual bodily harm — a
charge which today carries a maximum jail term of five years. One
person was given an IPP for "causing damage to an allotment."

*A handful of people are still in prison on IPPs for "summary motoring
offenses" — driving offenses so minor they could be tried in the
magistrates' courts without a jury.*

In the UK prisoners with good behaviour can often hope to serve half
their recommended term, meaning even those on a <u>mandatory life
sentence for murder</u> could be released in as little as seven-and-a-half
years. A guilty plea can also reduce sentence length. But VICE News
has found some IPP prisoners have spent a decade inside for crimes
described as "criminal damage and arson," or robbery.
The situation has been exacerbated by budget cutbacks to prisons,
probation, and the Parole Board, resulting in IPP prisoners becoming
trapped in the system.

John Samuels QC is a recently retired judge who sat on the parole
board for 10 years, and has been unable to talk publicly about the
IPP fiasco until now. Speaking exclusively to VICE News, he said that

IPP prisoners who have completed their recommended sentence should be released.

"Far more could be done, I have no doubt at all, in ensuring the safety of the public, by releasing those tariff-expired IPP sentences and supervising them effectively in the community, which would be cheaper and public safety would not be compromised," said Samuels.

"We've got a whole series of people who were caught up in indeterminate sentences who posed no danger to anyone — let alone society at large — and who are saddled with a need to remain in custody almost indefinitely."

But despite the ban on handing out IPP sentences, the situation is becoming progressively worse for those stuck inside.

In a "greasy spoon" cafe in Plymouth, southwest England, Michael Hood, 27, is showing off the many tattoos that adorn his body. They are the product of seven years spent in prison on an IPP. When he was 20, Hood was convicted of GBH with intent and was given an IPP sentence with a recommendation that he serve at least three years. Seven years later he was still in prison.

"At first I didn't really know what it was, then [other inmates] said 'Mate you just got a life sentence.' I said 'Nah I'll do three years' and they were like 'No mate, you'll be doing seven, eight, nine years before you get out of jail'… I was devastated," he said.

Hood was finally released a few months ago, but it was a struggle to get out.

He reels off the names of the courses he was required to do in a flurry of acronyms "CALM, PASRO, ETS, TSP, ARV," but maintains, "they're all the same. All they do is change the names of little things, but if you've done one course you can fly through the others."

But it was not as simple as doing one course after another. Hood was moved to nine different prisons in the space of seven years in order to get him on the right courses, and often faced long waiting lists.

VICE News examined prison inspection reports and used FOI requests to discover that many prisons do not run vital courses that IPP prisoners have been asked to complete. Of the 10 prisons with the highest IPP populations, only one ran the Alcohol Related Violence Program, for example.

At HMP Whatton, the prison that houses the most IPP prisoners, some people are left waiting for 14 months just to get onto one over-subscribed course. At another, HMP Wymott, inspectors found "insufficient places on offending behaviour programs and long waiting lists."
Required courses can also be added to a prisoner's sentence plan at any time, meaning the goalposts are constantly moving.

"It's a Catch-22," explained Juliet Lyon of the Prison Reform Trust, "if the only way you can demonstrate that you don't present a risk is to do courses, and the courses aren't available, or if you maintain your innocence you're not allowed to do the courses, or if you have mental health need or a learning disability you're still not allowed to do those courses... then you're completely stuck."

Cuts to the System

Even those that have completed all the courses required of them can face yet more barriers to release, as cuts to the budgets of prison officials and the Parole Board start to bite.
To get a release date, IPP prisoners need to persuade a three-member Parole Board panel that they pose no risk to society. Getting a proper hearing is not always easy, however.

Information revealed through FOI requests shows that the number of parole hearings that end up being deferred has almost quadrupled since 2010, even though the total number of hearings has dropped. More than a third of the 5,048 hearings that took place in 2014-15 were deferred. If this happens an application can go to the back of the line meaning a wait of months or even years.

Often the information provided to the Parole Board is inadequate. Many prisons are seriously overcrowded and the number of prison officers has reduced by 25 percent in the last five years.

That has left those responsible for overseeing IPP prisoners struggling. VICE News was shown a letter from an offender manager — the prison officer tasked with reviewing a prisoner's progress — explaining that huge cuts have left the service overwhelmed and unable to produce behaviour reports on time. These reports are relied upon when making decisions about a prisoner's future.

Samuels, the former judge, retired from the Parole Board on September 30. He told VICE News: "The backlog of cases before the Parole Board is growing all the time. In virtually every case I saw recently the panel was unable to conclude the review at the first hearing, because of deficiencies in what should have been included in the paperwork. So, cases are deferred shortly beforehand; or when the hearing takes place there is an adjournment.

"As a result of the Transforming Rehabilitation program, the probation service is in disarray. Prisoners often don't meet their offender manager until the parole hearing itself, and if they're lucky they will meet them for the first time over a video link," Samuels added.

VICE News calculated that the UK Ministry of Justice could save 119m pounds annually if it released IPP prisoners who have completed their mandatory minimum sentence, based on official estimates for the average annual cost of keeping prisoners in jail. The real figure is likely to be much higher due to the additional cost of rehabilitation courses, Parole Board hearings, and the cost of keeping prisoners on license for at least 10 years.

Life on Probation

For those that do make it past the required courses and the Parole Board, simply being released is not the end of the IPP story. Legislation stipulates all IPP prisoners will be on license for life, and could be recalled at any time.

VICE News found that of all the people released since the IPP sentence was banned in 2012, more than half have been recalled back to prison. In fact, last year alone, 330 IPP prisoners were recalled for breaching their probation — an average of six people a week.

In some cases, we found IPP prisoners being released on license only to be recalled for minor infractions of their probation terms. One man received an IPP sentence after being charged with sexual assault for grabbing a woman's behind in the line at the post office. After he was released he was recalled to prison after returning one night to his hostel drunk. He stayed in jail for 17 months until he could finally see the Parole Board and was released again.

And for some of those stuck in that system the uncertainty becomes too much.

Last year the number of IPPs reported as self-harming was equivalent to 42 percent of the total IPP population. Some go further. VICE News has found that since the sentences were abolished in 2012, at least 16 IPP prisoners have killed themselves while in jail. IPP prisoners are now more likely to die by suicide than prisoners with fixed release dates.

The Future

Legislation introduced in 2012 means that technically the justice secretary has the <u>power to change</u> any IPP sentence to a determinate one. But the Ministry of Justice told VICE News it had no plans to retroactively address the sentences of IPP prisoners, and stated that "the release of prisoners serving indeterminate sentences, imposed by the courts, is entirely a matter for the independent Parole Board."
If that remains the case, the release of IPP prisoners will continue at a painfully slow rate.

"The Parole Board, along with other agencies within the parole system are working hard to tackle the caseload, particularly demand for oral hearings which has increased considerably following the UK Supreme Court judgment [in 2013]," Glenn Gathercole, head of business development at the Parole Board, told VICE News.

"I'm not saying I didn't deserve prison, because I did," added Hood. "What I done weren't a nice thing. What I didn't deserve was a sentence with no release date."

The latest figures from the Ministry of justice shows at the end of June 2016, there were 11,359 (10,992 male; 367 female) indeterminate sentenced prisoners (those serving Imprisonment for Public Protection (IPP) sentences and life sentences) in the prison population. This represents a drop of 6% compared to June 2015.

As a result of the abolition of the IPP sentence in 2012, offenders are no longer receiving these sentences and prisoners are only being released or recalled. Consequently, the decrease in the indeterminate sentenced population can be explained almost entirely by the declining IPP population

There were fewer than 4,000 (3,998) IPP prisoners as at 30 June 2016. This represents a drop of 34% since the June 2012 peak of 6,080. Over the last twelve months alone, the IPP population has reduced by more than 600 (13%). The proportion of the IPP population who are post-tariff continues to increase; 82% of IPP prisoners are now post-tariff compared to 77% this time last year.

Whilst these figures are to be welcomed there are still too many genuine cases of IPP prisoners who are still caught up in the system. Many IPP Sentenced Prisoners cannot get on the courses to address their offending behaviour through lack of resources within the system. This causes further injustice to the prisoner and their families.

Chapter Two Case of Shaun Lloyd

Ms Lloyd who set up the IPP Campaign in Wales and mother of
Shaun Lloyd was one of the campaigners who got a petition signed
by 500 people to release her son who was given a IPP sentence, and
took it to Downing street calling on politicians to release her son
Shaun, who was sent to prison for street robbery when he was aged
18 in 2006.

Shaun had by then had done nearly 3 times the recommended Tariff
set by the trial judge even though Shaun had shown remorse for his
crime and completed all his courses they still deemed him not fit for
release.

Ms Lloyd admitted her son was no angel and excepted what he did was wrong however she felt that IPP sentences was supposed to be meant for rapists and paedophiles. Miss Lloyd protested outside the House of Commons and later met up with Jenny Rathbone to hand in her petition.

Ms Lloyd said She felt there was no light at the end of the tunnel and have days where she felt she was having a breakdown. She went on to say how difficult it was to visit her son who was so far away from home.

Ms Jenny Rathbone Am told reporters at the time that the fact that IPPs have now been abolished confirms that they are not appropriate for delivering justice. It is a pity that Parliament failed to make the Act retrospective as it now leaves people like Shaun Lloyd in Legal limbo. Shaun has already served his time for his offence. It is commendable that his family is fighting for justice for Shaun and all the other people left in no man's Land.

Ms Lloyd didn't stop there she took her campaign to the Welsh Assembly in 2013 and made her voice heard. Ms Jenny Rathbone attended the event and fully supported her in her fight too free Shaun. The campaign to free Shaun was also getting a fair bit of media coverage too and the campaign was growing.

Ms Lloyd continued her campaign for her son and in 2014 Shaun went against his Solicitors, Offenders Management who recommended Shaun go to an open prison (Shaun had been to open prisons on two occasion previously and had let him down) and argued his case before the parole board and pleaded for his own release. Shaun was released from prison two weeks later on the 17th of February 2014. It does go to show that sometimes the parole board will listen to the inmate's reasons and release them accordingly like they did with Shaun.

Ms Lloyd and her son Shaun actively campaign for others to be released from the IPP sentences and Shaun knows the effects IPP sentences have on those left behind and their families.

Shaun and his mother are now taking on government ministers with a view to getting the sentences of the 4500 Prisoners with IPP sentences converted and or abolished.

It is excepted that if a prisoner commits a crime he deserves a prison sentence however to give someone a sentence with no release date is inhumane. Shaun says he knew prisoners who killed themselves because of the IPP sentences they were given and want to fight for the remaining prisoners because who will if he doesn't? I can't forget about it because of the consequences – Its life or death.

Shaun has got married and now has a child. Many people as they get older do change and I believe many of the IPP prisoners left behind could turn their lives around if they were given the chance. I do hope the government after hearing the plight of IPP prisoners and their families will do the right thing and release all IPP prisoners with time served.

Any prisoner who spend years in prison are normally damaged by their experience and suffer some form or Post traumatic stress disorder. It's important that the government makes sure there is help given to all IPP prisoners upon release too.

Another case through Ms Lloyds campaign which was brought to my attention was that of Kiya Smith.

Chapter Three– Case of Kiya Smith

Kiya Smith was just 17 years old when he was given an IPP sentence for a street robbery which consisted of stealing a mobile phone and £7.00 in cash. His previous convictions were of petty thefts and nothing in his previous history to warrant such a harsh sentence.

Kiya was sentenced by the trial judge to a tariff of 2 years however he is still in prison 3 years over his tariff and is on his sixth year. Kiya will be 23 in January 2017.

One of the problems Kiya faced was trying to do the courses in relation to his offending behaviour there are 9 courses he has to complete before the parole board will consider him for release, however they kept moving him to different prisons five in total so he could not complete the courses. He started off at the Park Prison in Bridgend, Swinton Hall, Hewell Grange, Long Lartin and ended up in Frankland Prison.

Kiya was moved without any warning from Long Lartin and his family had already bought train tickets to go to visit him.

This frustrated Kiya and the last straw for him was when he was moved to Frankland Prison near the Scottish border so far away from his family making it very difficult to have visits.

Kiya had enough and placed himself down the segregation unit to try and get a move out of this prison. He has been in the segregation for 5 months and most penal reformers and ex-prisoners will tell you this takes a toll on your mental health. Being locked up 23 hours a day and if you're lucky and it's not raining you may get an hour out of your cell for exercise.

As I write this book Kiya is having a hard time and on the 24th of July 2016, between 9.15 and 9.40am alleges he was assaulted by several officers they came into his cell in the segregation unit and restrained him. Kiya goes on to say one prison officer in particular placed his hands around his throat to strangle him. Kiya said he lost consciousness and when he came around this one officer was hitting him in the face.

Two other prisoners were subjected to similar assaults. I have seen the letter from their lawyers who have made a complaint about these incidents.

The injuries sustained by Kiya and the other two prisoners has nothing to do with restraining them and is inconsistent with the injuries they sustained. This is just blatant abuse of prisoners being beaten up.

A tactic used against the prisoner to justify these beatings was to turn the tables on them and the prison officer/s then blamed the prisoner for assaulting them and placed them on false charges of assault. They have done this with Kiya and two other prisoners. I saw these tactics used in nearly all the prisons I was in and they usually always got away with it. Governors rarely go against there own officers for fear of a staff walking out and usually find the prisoner guilty of offences they haven't done.

Having served time in Frankland prison myself it was a common occurrence to regularly beat prisoners up when I was there and that was 19 years ago. I also brought it to the authority's attention in my previous book in 2012 what was going on in Frankland Prison yet nothing has been done about It.

Letters to the prisoners down the segregation always seem to take a few weeks to get them they get them in the evening rather than in the day and Kiya has had this problem.

Kiya does not go looking for trouble all he wanted was to complete the courses so he can go before the parole board and go home to his family. Moving him from prison to prison has not helped him and the courses he needs to do there are a long waiting list of approximately 6 to 8 months. How can the authorities justify this and why hasn't Kiya been sent to the prisons which actually does the courses? This is what you would call a breach of natural justice. Unless the Authorities send Kiya and other prisoners to the right places to do these courses they are left in limbo and cannot get a release date.

There's also the issue of why Kiya is so far away from his family it's been proven time and time again that family ties are important to reduce the risk of reoffending how can he keep those family ties going when he is nearly 300 miles away from his loved ones?

Kiya has saved up his visiting orders so he can get accumulated visits however at every turn the authorities block him from going to Cardiff, Swansea or any other prison nearer to home stating that the prisons will not except him.

Kiya has a young daughter who is now aged 6 and has not been able to keep in contact with her as much as he would like because he's so far away. she is always asking when is daddy coming home.

I do wonder whether it could be argued that Kiya mum and family right to family life has been breached?

Kiya's mum Donna Wall said she was heartbroken when her son first got this IPP sentence she said paedophiles get a lesser sentence and it isn't fair at all. I worry all the time I might get a phone call to say my son has hurt himself and since this sentence was imposed It has affected me in everyday life and my families.

I'm on Medication for severe depression since this all happened and cry a lot and break down not knowing when he is going to come home and be free its mental torture. Its affected all the family.

Photos of Kiya Smith

Chapter four Case of David Magee

David Magee was given a IPP sentence in 2007 for wounding with intent on a male when he was 19 years old his tariff given by the judge was 2 years and 10 days. David has been moved to a number of different prisons over the years and even made it to category D prisons however things didn't work out for him there and he was recalled for not going back to the hostel he was meant to be staying in and got recalled once because of drinking.

David is now 29 and has done 8 years over the tariff recommended by the trial judge. David has found it difficult to stay in contact with his family and has refused to see them on some occasions as he feels it makes his time go longer and finds it hard to cope with.

David is now in Warren Hill 300 miles away from his family and does not know what the future holds with no release date forthcoming.

David's family have said that they find it very difficult to visit him because they feel they are doing the sentence with him. David's sister Claire explained that after the visit has finished the nice feeling of seeing him was short lived as I felt really down for the next few days, a comedown as such. I assume it is because he is so far away and I hated leaving him there not knowing when he was going to be released.

David has made significant progress in that he has now completed all the courses he's been asked to do Some time ago. You have to ask the question why he is still in prison when he is no long a risk to the public?

David's Mum, said,

"I have missed out on so much on the years my son has spent in prison, it's upsetting when I see the fine young men his friends have turned into with families of their own and having good jobs whilst my son has been deprived of all this, many people do not know I even got a son which I find very depressing and upsetting. All we want is my son back home so he can rebuild his family life that he deserves. We are only asking for a chance for this to happen"

David's Dad said,

"It's a day I will never forget. That phone call changed my life. "Dad, I got two years IPP" It was a kick in the balls times 10. I knew IPP. I knew the damage and knew the impact. I've done time myself. David was living with me at the time, it sounds shit to say this but I knew I'd lost my boy to jail. HMP was his life now. It's a nasty nasty sentence. Nout worse. My boy is a forgotten prisoner."

There may be some glimmer of hope for David in that his parole board hearing is due in November. Claire his sister is optimistic that her brother will finally be released soon and they are feeling a lot more positive for the future than they were previously.

When you look at the length of time David has done it shows a damming inditement of our criminal justice system when you consider that many prisoner's get less for Murder, Manslaughter and Sexual offences. How can this be deemed a fair sentence?

David Magee (in grey top) and his family

David Magee and his sister Claire Bown

Chapter Five Case of Craig Inskip

In 2001 Craig Inskip came to the authority's attention after having a lot of issues with school and later committing petty criminal offences. Craig on his third offence which was classed as robbery. He was brought before the court to answer for stealing two mobile phones and 40 pounds in cash.

The trial Judge sentenced Craig aged 21 years old to an IPP sentence and was given a tariff of over 18 months. This sentence in theory should have seen Craig released back into society by the age of 23 however now aged 30 years of age Craig is still locked up in the system without any hope of a release date even though Craig has completed all the courses he had to do. Craig is now 7 years and approximately six months over his trial tariff.

Craig's has had to endure the death of his father who committed suicide because of the case and who never got over the fact his son went to prison. On this occasion, they allowed Craig to go to the funeral to pay his respects.

Craig suffered another blow sometime later when his sister died but on this occasion, was not allowed to go to the funeral. Craig felt there was no reasonable explanation for this.

Craig's mental health deteriorated as a result of all this and found it difficult to cope. Recently Craig has faced further criminal charges in relation to selling legal highs in prison and was brought before the courts without any legal representation due to the cut backs in legal aid according to his family and was later found guilty and given a 7 year 8-month sentence. Craig protests his innocence and feels he has been done a further injustice to what he's already had.

Craig must serve the 7 years and 8-month sentence before he can be considered for parole. In relation to the IPP sentence he will have to serve this after the five years has expired.

Craig mum said,

When Craig got his sentence we both thought he would be serving the 18 months it wasn't until about a year into that we started to look into this IPP we didn't even know it was an I

Ipp, or what the IPP actually entailed! We were stunned the whole family his father told me we're never going to get him back it's a life sentence.

It tore our family apart his father commuted suicide we were not getting visits they were and still are forever moving him, I've not seen him for over two years, I booked a visit in March even though my health is bad and they moved him from Liverpool to Staffordshire days before my visit.

Craig protested and didn't want to go!! They went in his cell in full riot gear and beat my son badly he had several broken ribs, I complained and nothing was done, he's been injured and slashed for his property his life is hell in prison, as is ours out here, he asked for accumulated visits because of my health, the prison rang me about it and I explained it all to them and was told they arrange it Asap!

I'm still waiting more than six months on!! I have a secreting tumour on my pituitary gland it's called lymphocytic hypophysis it's stop my kidneys working, also cushiness syndrome during that treatment my heart became ill I had a triple heart bypass which failed! I developed severe arthritis and to top it off development lung problems and now have emphysema and coped so my health has deteriorated badly.

Craig started going downhill rapidly after his father died he had a break down in prison and attempted to hang himself and recently self-harmed and slashed himself, he is half the lad I knew, I asked the prison to have him assessed for ADHD nothing again and also about this odd sound he makes when talking to him I'm sure it's the onset to torretts.

It's a constant worry and I know my life Is short now I worry that I may die when he's in prison and he's says that I'm all he lives for and that he will commit suicide if I die! It kills my heart that would be all my family gone, I had 4 children Craig is all I have left now, I just want my child back before prison kills him.

Craig said, the day will come when I am free, then it will be my turn to forget those who forgot me, forgotten in a cage without a key!!

Chapter Six case of Prisoner A

Due to legal reason's I cannot name this prisoner so will call him prisoner A. Prisoner A was convicted of sexual offences in 2007 and was given a IPP sentence.

Prisoner A received a tariff of 9 years reduced to eight on appeal however like most IPP sentenced prisoners he is now over his tariff set by the trial judge.

The problems prisoner A faces because he is maintaining he did not do the crimes he was convicted of is that he cannot do any of the courses without an admission of guilt and he would not do that as he knows he is innocent.

In relation to IPP sentences it is interesting to note that the first application for Parole is normally rejected and as I write this book have found no IPP prisoners who won parole first time around.

The Parole board cannot either deal with a prisoner saying he is innocent and more likely than not refuse parole to any prisoner maintaining their innocence with the mindset that they cannot evaluate if the prisoner is a risk to the public.

Kenneth Clarke the former Home Secretary conceded it was impossible for a prisoner to prove he was not a risk to the public so it has to be said where does this leave Prisoner A and many other prisoners protesting their innocence?

Prisoner A is an ex veteran and is coping better than most prisoners however his wife believes this is down to how the army taught him to survive. prisoner A health has suffered like many others and he has had a heart attack whilst in prison.

How many prisoners who are on IPP sentences and are claiming they are innocent are unknown due to the authorities not keeping records of this but one thing is for sure prisoner A is not the only one and there are many more.

It will be interesting to see how the system deals with these type of prisoners and whether they will be penalised more than they already have been. In relation to the basic standard and enhanced regimes it has been known for those who protest their innocence to be excluded from being allowed enhanced status just for refusing to admit guilt. In effect being punished for the same offence twice.

Under article 6.1 of the European Human Rights Convention it states everyone is entitled to a fair hearing and I do wonder if the hearings of many prisoners which go before the parole board on IPP to access whether they are fit for release are actual getting a fair hearing because they protest their innocence. The Government must look at these cases with an open mind and give prisoners hope of being released.

An announcement on the Parole Board's website states that: 'A myth has grown up that unless a prisoner admits and expresses remorse for the crime that they have been sentenced for, they will not get parole. This is not true.' In support of their argument, the Parole Board list five points that they say disprove the existence of the parole deal. In this short article, I consider each of the Parole Board's points in turn and show that they do not disprove the parole deal they actually prove that prisoners who maintain their innocence and refuse to go on offending behaviour programmes are less likely to be released.

First, the Parole Board acknowledge that it would be unlawful to refuse parole solely on the grounds of denial of guilt or not being able to take part in offending behaviour programmes which focus on the crime committed. In the same breath, however, they state that despite this: 'The Board is bound to take account not only of the offence, and the circumstances in which it was committed, but the circumstances and behaviour of the individual prisoner before and during the sentence.'

This entirely undermines any notion that the Parole Board takes seriously the existence of innocent prisoners. It gives hope to prisoners maintaining innocence that they have an equal chance in law of achieving freedom with prisoners who were guilty of the offences for which they were convicted. It, then, demolishes that hope by insisting that they must take account not only of the offence for which they were wrongly convicted but, also, their behaviour during their sentence.

Second, the parole board argue that 'it is important to understand that the board is not entitled to "go behind" the conviction and overrule the decision of a judge or jury. This is because 'the Board's remit extends only to the assessment of risk, and the bottom line is always the safety of the public.'

I do not know of anyone who would expect the parole board to overrule the decisions of the courts. That would be a truly bizarre situation. But, the way in which they hide behind their organisational remit and refuse to acknowledge the reality of innocent prisoners cannot be justified. The courts are not infallible. Wrongful imprisonment can, and does, occur, not only for crimes that innocent men and women did not, in fact, commit, but, also, for crimes that did not, even, occur. This fact has been proven in dozens of high profile cases that have been overturned in the Court of Appeal – Stephen Downing, Robert Brown, Sally Clark, Sheila Bowler, Patrick Nichols, Kevin Callan, and so on.

Third, the parole board report that 'the figures back in 2003 show that in 24% of cases where prisoners maintained their innocence, parole was granted. This compares with 51% of all applications granted. This shows, according to the parole board, that the belief that "if you don't admit the crime, you don't get parole" is patently untrue.'

The problem with the statistics presented is that whilst they do show that some innocent prisoners achieve a parole licence, at the same time they actually emphasise that prisoners who maintain their innocence are less likely to achieve parole – they have half as much chance. This does not dispel the 'parole deal' it proves it!
Fourth, the Parole Board employs a particularly perverse logic. They say that their 'core task of assessing the risk of future harm to the public is often made more difficult when dealing with those who deny guilt. This is because there may simply be less information to go on, particularly where the prisoner has not been able to undertake any relevant offending behaviour work. Detailed reports of a wide range of offending behaviour programmes are a key source of information for Board members in working out how a prisoner operates and copes with life and therefore what the risk to the public

of a future offence might be.'

This shifts the focus of why prisoners who maintain their innocence are less likely to be recommended for parole to the victims of wrongful imprisonment themselves. It blames them for their own failure to comply with the needs of the Board and undertake relevant offending behaviour courses and provide the detailed information to assist Board members in their deliberations. This brings the parole deal into clear view and puts prisoners who maintain their innocence in an impossible catch-22 position. The only realistic way of achieving release is to acknowledge that they are murderers or rapists or sex abusers and work with prison staff on that aspect of their behaviour, even if they are not.

Finally, the parole board rely on further statistical evidence in the form of a breakdown of 50 release cases recommended by the board. 'The fifty were all serving mandatory life sentences for murder. Of these, nine had maintained their innocence in whole or in part throughout their sentence.'

Again, this reference to statistics only serves to further strengthen the concern that prisoners who maintain their innocence are at a disadvantage in terms of parole board decisions. This is because the survey cited decreases the statistical average from 24% of successful applicants to the parole board in 2003 who maintained their innocence to a maximum of 18% of the mandatory life prisoners surveyed.

This figure is decreased still further when it is taken into account that an unknown of the 18% referred to did not maintain their innocence for the whole of their sentences, but only part of it. As a final insight into the mind-set of the parole board, it is interesting to note that the majority of the mandatory lifers who were recommended for parole, whether or not they maintained their innocence, had conceded their guilt and undertaken offending behaviour courses. This leaves us none the wiser and raises the crucial question: How many of the 9 mandatory lifers who the Parole Board recommended should be released did maintain their innocence for the whole of their sentences and did not attend offending behaviour programmes?

Whatever the parole board might say, then, they have not provided any evidence to support the claim that the parole deal is a 'myth'. On the contrary, the evidence that they put forward actually proves that the parole deal does exist. Prisoners who maintain their innocence and are unable to take part in offending behaviour programmes because they have no offending behaviour to confront are less likely to be considered for parole than offenders who admit their guilt and comply with the requirements of the prison and parole regimes. (by Dr Michael Naughton.) First appeared in inside times Newspaper.

Prisoners maintaining innocence are held to ransom.

It is clear to many within the system, that as prisons and psychology departments are funded via the provision of courses, rather than the successful process of offenders; there is a perverse incentive to generate income by not progressing offenders, but continuously adding further hurdles to cross.

With the increasing number of prisoners maintaining innocence, offenders with indeterminate sentences or those awaiting parole post-tariff are literally 'a captive population' for prisons to hold onto for income.

By allowing convictions in our courts on uncorroborated hearsay the prison population is rising and the costs are spiralling out of control. There is little or no evidence of benefit to SOTP courses, but those delivering these courses have a vested interest. Those prisoners maintaining their innocence are harassed and held to ransom in order to undertake courses despite statistical evidence that they already have a lower risk of reoffending than those who complete the programmes. It should also be noted that the founder of these programmes (Canada) has stopped courses of this nature, followed by America, as they are 'not fit for purpose'. Which is their statement!

I would suggest that when psychologist's cosy up and suggest you do more courses, you should ask the following questions:

1) What cognitive defects do you claim that I have? These pins them down and makes them explain whether you actually need the course to reduce your risk, or are they just after bums-on-seats. Once they give you a list of deficits you should ask:

2) Is the person who is claiming I have these deficits qualified to do so? What are their qualifications and do they have any specialist knowledge of forensic psychology? It is an offence for them to claim abilities that they do not have. Forensic psychology is a specialist field, and most prison psychologists are not qualified to practise it.

3) Ask them to explain exactly how these deficits are related to your offending. They could, and do, give prisoners lists of deficits that have no connection to your offending behaviour. Beware of the words 'may benefit'.

4) Ask for the background paperwork for the course, the course assessment criteria and the course selection criteria. You must be in a position to give properly informed consent.

5) Ask for any evidence that the course will actually address your deficits.

6) Ask for the possible negative consequences of taking part in the course?

These questions are taken directly from the British Psychological Society – code of ethics and offending behaviours; every prisoner is entitled to have a copy of this document and should make the necessary enquiries with their solicitor to obtain a copy, or write to the British Psychological Society, 48 Princess Road East, Leicester, LE1 7DR. (Written by B Stanford Wymott Prison).

Chapter Seven - case of John Cotter

John Cotter was only 22 when he was given an IPP sentence for Manslaughter what is unusual about this case is John did not have any convictions prior to this case and sentencing prisoners to IPP normally only occurs if he had previous convictions for a violent offence. John did not have any. This in itself goes against the sentencing guidelines under IPP.

Secondly John has always protested his innocence and was convicted under the Joint Enterprise Law. John was given a 15-year tariff by the trial judge and to date has served 10 years of this sentence.

When John was told I was writing this book he sent me a letter via his partner setting out what it is like for him being a IPP prisoner and for the others who are in there under this sentence.

My name is John William Cotter and I understand that you are doing a book about IPP prisoners and our treatment. Well I would like to thank you for letting me be part of it and there is so much I would like to say to you. I am not really good at doing letters but will try my best to put something down for you to put in your book. If you would like to come up and see me so I can tell you in words it would be much better because I am a good talker not writer. Just let my misses Steph know and it could be sorted out.

I was given a IPP of 7 years in 2008 because of the joint enterprise law. I was told unless I was going to give evidence against my two co-defendants then I would be convicted of murder with them both, never mind I was not even in the same room when the attack took place but I was never going to give evidence against them for many of my own reasons.

One of the reasons I was still only a boy of 23 and did not see or know what I know now being 33! So when we went to court at The Old Bailey there was a basis upon pleas offered of Manslaughter but only if all three of us took it there and then. So, when I spoke to my legal team they said if I was not going to give evidence against my two co-defendants there was a good chance I would be convicted of murder because of joint enterprise law. In my eyes, I had no choice but to plead guilty to Manslaughter to save my co-defendants and stop the chance of all of us going away for murder and getting a really long time.

Little did I know I was going to go away for a very long time anyway by being given an IPP for my first time in jail? How unfair is that? Given IPP but never been to jail even in my life!!

My two co-defendants did not confess to who used the knife when we were sentenced so the Judge said "There were three of you present when this attack took place upon a man who was on his own and completely at your mercy". I was not present, I was in another room and then he goes on to say "I note that even now not one of you accepts responsibility for removing his ear or inflicting the fatal injury upon him". I was not in the room when the attack took place so how was I meant to say who did it? And even if I did know who did it then it was not up to me to say so it was up to my co-defendant who used the knife, but he was never going to own up to it in court that day so the Judge said "I see no reason to make any distinction between any of you, for in my judgement your responsibility for this grave offence is joint!". He then sentenced us all to the same sentence of Imprisonment of Public Protection minimum period of 8 years! I have never been to jail before, my co-defendants have for GBH but I haven't and the Judge still gave me the same sentence.

It's only now that my co-defendant Ricky Beesley has owned up to using the knife. He told those in authority and wrote a confession to being the sole attacker and in the confession, he has stated that I was not even in the same room when the attack took place, but still 11 years later I am still in jail and can't get home as an innocent man? But that is the justice system for IPPs? It's mad and a flawed system, it is an unfair toxic sentence that is killing men and women all the time in prison. Some people have got an IPP for silly reasons but have done 11, 12 years? The likes of Charlie Richardson and The Krays they had done that sort of time but they made millions and hurt and killed so many people, they were notorious criminals! Most of us IPPs are not those people sirs but we are doing the same time as them sort of people? How can that be right? This is so unjust and inhumane for us to be treated like animals. Having no release date? Even the worse criminals in the world have had release dates!

And the prisons are not helping at all, they don't give a shit at all. Like the jail I am in now HMP Stoken all they want to do is keep you in prison, no progression, no help and no programmes. We are money to them, the longer we stay the more money they get because an IPP can be here for years and they love that. I feel after doing nearly 11 years and all the offending behaviour programmes you can do and jumping through hoops they have asked am I now closer to going home? How is that right when I have never had D Cat and I am three years over tariff? I am at a point where I am losing it, I am a really strong man but I am starting to lose it and feel like giving up. Some days I would love to take my own life because I see no hope, no light, no help and these Prison Officers don't give a shit. They go out of their way to push my buttons so they can write SRI's in my nomis, so they can keep me in jail. They are kids, most of the Officers now between the ages of 18-24? They were children/teenagers when I started this sentence and don't know what an IPP is? I am getting mad every day, I have gone passed the point of caring now because I feel like why should I carry on jumping through hoops and getting nothing back from these people. When you get a new dog and want it to do tricks you have to give the dog something i.e. treats or something or it won't do tricks for you, why are we all going to keep doing everything they ask but get nothing but knock back after knock back from them?

Why are we are being kept in jail for something we 'might' do when or if we are released? This is a joke and an impossible task to prove to them. They could put any body in prison for something they might do! They could throw anyone in prison and ask them to prove they won't do something when they are released. Who knows what anybody in this world might do at any day or time and ex prisoner or normal Joe Blogs? I am sick of trying, sick of waking up in the morning in these places. Sometimes before I go to sleep I pray I don't wake up! Because this is not living, but I have got to try for my family, my little girl and my misses but I feel that I haven't got much more knock backs in me sir. I feel there is no hope as an IPP, one of the highest rates of self-harm is by IPPs. Figures show that for every 1000 people serving IPPs, 550 have self-harmed. I know people, many of people who have took their own life because of the IPP, where is our human rights?

Our families are doing the sentence just as much as us, is it right for them to never know if we will ever come home? Sometimes I feel that if I died it would be better for them because they could bury me and move on with their lives and not worry anymore? I have written to MPs and begged and asked for help and none have helped? The parole board are not seeing that this sentence is not helping me now it is making me worse. We can't get home because of them, we get delays for boards and they are sometimes over a year delays! A lack of available place on offending behaviour programmes is that our fault? no! a lack of available resources and poor managing procedures, is that our fault? no! So why and how can they keep us in jail years beyond our original tariff without knowing when we will be released? I feel that we must be animals because this sentence was abolished in 2012 as it is against human rights so what does that make us then? This is a nightmare and I wish I knew what I know now that day in court as then I would not have plead guilty and went to trial for murder instead because even murderers have release dates.

No public really know about IPPs because the system has hidden it well. I want people to know what these people are doing to us and our families. And now because I am in love with an ex officer I met at The Mount Prison they are coming after me nonstop. Trying their best to keep me in here, it never stops for me here at Stoken. They have been voted the third worse prison in the country! They have taken me away from my family 250miles away and will not transfer me closer to home when all I do is put transfer forms in? I am being threatened by Officers and bullied by them, they make false reports about me, things that never even happened? They make believe stuff apparently, I had said or done? And when I put complaints in saying about their behaviour they do nothing. I have put in 44 complaints in here in the past seven months and all they do is cover up their bullshit? I have even tried to get Leicester Police involved but they said they can't help? To me no because my girlfriend was an Officer they hate it and me so how am I ever going to get home? After nearly 11 years I am now going to be kept in jail for being in love?

I hope this helps you with the book and if you need any more stuff then please just ask Steph and I will sort it out. I hope you can help me and others in jail as IPPs because we are the FORGOTTEN PRISONERS!

Two significant developments have occurred recently in that the law has changed on Joint enterprise which may help John with a new appeal and just as important his co accused have wrote a letter and told the authorities that John had no involvement in the murder whatsoever and John has never wavered from what he said at trial.

John is hoping for a new appeal and is currently seeking barrister's advice however this sentence has had a massive impact on his life and his families.

Stephanie Lauder Johns Partner said,

I have only known my partner John for a year and a half but for this short time I have seen the effect this sentence has on John and his family. John never committed the crime he is in for plus he has never been in prison before so for him to spend ten years inside has been really hard for him and his family. Right now, we are fighting for him to come home but like the rest of the forgotten IPPs he feels like the system has let him down and wonders if he ever will get released.

Recently he has expressed to me how depressed he is, telling me what's the point and how he should do us all a favour and kill himself this kills me inside! What about his and other prisoner's human rights? They have abolished this sentenced year ago so why can't they let them have another shot in life and release these poor people? John was 22 when he went inside and is nothing like the person he once was. Hopefully this book will help the forgotten IPPs and make people understand that enough is enough.

Chapter Eight- Case of James Ward

James Ward was serving a prison sentence for ABH and was given a 12-month sentence for this offence, He got into a scuffle with his father, Bill, over the family dog and lashed out. His father said he was full of remorse right after the incident and said it was the worst thing he had ever done and that he was a good lad.

Whilst in prison and near to the end of his sentence unable to cope and adjust to prison Life, James set fire to his cell mattress (A common occurrence in prisons). James was then placed on report and disciplined for this via the prison disciplinary system.

When he had completed his sentence, upon James release he was gated arrested by the police and taken to the police station where he was questioned and later charged with arson with intent to endanger life in relation to setting fire to his mattress in his cell.

James was brought before the courts at the age of 19 and was given an IPP sentence and was given a low tariff of 18- months.

Whilst in Prison James did all the courses he was asked to do and sometimes did them more than once and did courses which were even irrelevant to him.

Now into his tenth year of his sentence the Parole Board have heard James case for parole on three separate occasions yet have still refused to release him on the sole basis they cannot determine if he is still a danger to the public.

A former Home Secretary abolished the IPP sentences in 2012 stating that it was impossible for prisoners to prove they were no longer a risk to the public and was the reason he abolished this Act. The Parole Board should have been aware of what the Home Secretary has said at James parole hearings and it does appear they are keeping him in prison with no sound basis for doing so. James has no release date and feels there is no hope for him being released anytime soon.

James told Zoe Conway reporter, For BBC Radio 4 Today who has reported on IPP sentences in her programme that he found prison hard to cope with, being trapped in a box.

"Prison is not fit to accommodate people like me with mental health problems. It's made me worse. How can I change in a place like this? I wake up every morning scared of what the day may hold"

James regularly self-harms, sets light to his cell, barricades himself in and has staged dirty protests. With a low IQ, and suffering mental health problems, he clearly cannot cope with prison life.

James has set light to his cell several times. His solicitor, Pippa Carruthers, says it is linked to his mental health.

"He becomes overwhelmed," she says. "He loses sight of what he needs to do to prove to a parole board that he is no longer a risk and he acts destructively."

James family have been very concerned about his health and their worse fear is getting a phone call from the prison to say that Jimmy had killed himself.

James' mother, father and sister visited him recently in prison. They said they were worried by his appearance describing him as "lost and confused".

The Parole Board has not reviewed James' case for over two years and because the system has failed to carry out a required psychological and psychiatric assessment of him, it could be another year before he gets another parole board hearing.

He could be in prison for several more years.

James said he felt like he was "rotting" in the prison system.

James in my opinion is suffering from what is known as post-traumatic stress disorder having suffered with it myself for nearly 20 years I see the signs and it is a very bad mental health problem which the authorities need to look at after all they owe James a duty of care.

My own experiences have shown that The prison authorities cannot deal with mental health problems very well of prisoners and there is clear evidence there for all to see why James mental health has deteriorated and that is because of the unjust imprisonment and length of time he has done.

James has watched rapists and paedophiles serve lesser sentences than he has done and watched them be released time and time again. I think that is enough to mess anyone's head up. The IPP System was set up for rapists and paedophiles like them. Not for petty crimes like James was in for and it makes a total mockery of the system when things like this happen.

It should be noted that James was already disciplined by the prison authorities for setting his fire to his mattress and then dealt with again by the police. This in my view is punishing someone for the same offence twice which is forbidden under the European Courts of Humans. Protocol 7 Article 4.1 States no one shall be liable to be tried twice for the same offence.

Recently a man from Swansea set fire to his prison cell has avoided another jail term after a judge ruled it would be "like throwing a match into a can of petrol".

Ian Graham set fire to his cell, damaged property and attacked a prison officer while at Hmp Swansea after making threats to a local authority worker. He was jailed for eight weeks back last year.

The incident caused the officer to take four weeks off work due to an injury to his knee, and an estimated repair bill for his cell of up to £2,000.

Ian Graham had pleaded guilty to arson, criminal damage and assault on a prison custody officer on the day of his trial, and returned to Court for sentencing.

Mitigating, Mark Davies said he did not agree with the recommendation in a pre-sentence report that Graham should face a custodial sentence.

He said: "I totally understand the recommendations; however, I do not think it is in his interests."

He added: "When left alone he does not really bother anyone. When he can't deal with situations he gets upset and angry. He has only left Wales once in his life.

"He spent time locked in his cell in Swansea Prison, when that stress appeared to turn into aggression."

District Judge Steve Harmes sentenced Graham to 26 weeks to run consecutively, suspended for two years.

He said: "You are an unusual figure to see in court. You are 55 years old and have committed two or three offences, and gone to prison.

"I am sympathetic to you. You have difficulties in your life, however, you can't behave like this. You put people in danger when you start a fire. You have to be punished for that.

"Each offence passes a criminal threshold but...putting you back in prison not only may make you unwell, it will create risks."

He added: "Should I throw a match into a can of petrol, it may be what I am doing throwing you into custody."

Graham was also ordered to pay a total of £1,789, a combination of compensation for damages caused to the prison, a victim surcharge, and £250 compensation to the prison officer he injured.

When you look at both of these cases it clearly shows the injustice which has been done to James and why he feels very aggrieved.

Graham committed worse offences than James did and his sentence was suspended. how can James sentence be justified and the time he has served when you compare it to the case of Graham? It's interesting to note the judges' comments in the Graham case because they could easily apply to James case and I quote them for ease of reference here.

"I am sympathetic to you. You have difficulties in your life, however, you can't behave like this. You put people in danger when you start a fire. You have to be punished for that.

"Each offence passes a criminal threshold but...putting you back in prison not only may make you unwell, it will create risks."

This is the whole point in James case the length of time he has been in prison has made him unwell due to suffering post-traumatic stress disorder and the only way James is going to get better is for him to be released from that environment. Leaving James in prison will only damage his mental health further.

James clearly deserves another chance and I hope at the next parole hearing that James will get his parole. James has a loving family to come home to and has a safety net where he will get all the support he needs to adjust to outside life. James even has a job to go to for when he is released. What more evidence do the parole board need to see that James should be released?

Jamie's family on the campaign trail

Ellie right , Mia to the left

James family on the campaign trail

James sister April Ward

James with his mum and Dad

James and his sister April. April says growing up together, we had a great childhood. I always looked up to James. He would always look out for me and was a very caring, loving big brother.

Aspiring footballer James. James loved playing football and lots of other outdoor activities. James was in the cadets and was one of the top in his group! When he was 16 he applied for the army which was he's dream job. James failed his medical due to pins in his arms from an accident he had in his teens which meant James could not join the army.

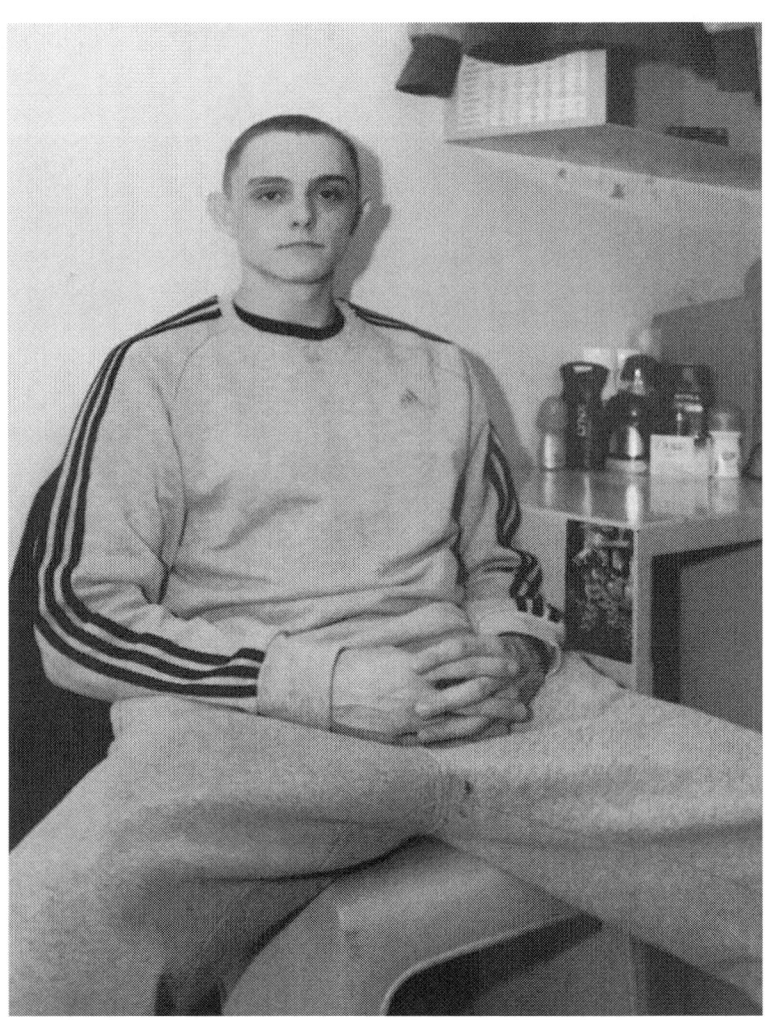

James

These are comments from James family to show how IPP has affected their lives and still is having a massive impact on them.

James Niece said,

Before the IPP came into my life I had a close bond with my uncle James he would tuck me in bed and read me stories, take me to the park, I was always with him every minute I could. He always made sure I was safe and having lots of fun. When he was taken away our bond grew distant. For the first 6 to 7 years for him being in side I could only write he didn't want me seeing him in that place or going through the searches just to see him with all the other prisoners ' thinking it may upset me.

When I was 14 I was finally allowed to go, and wow the change he was a different person the close bond was gone. He wasn't the man I remembered and I wasn't the little pain he remembered.

The first visit was hard and yes it was upsetting. Now I go more regular but still not wanting to say too much about my life because I don't want to upset James. We have both missed out on 10 years we will never get back. It's heart-breaking.

April James Sister said,

We would visit James every 2 weeks, when 5 years into James's 10 months Ipp sentence I had a little girl called Ellie, at first I wasn't sure if I wanted my new born baby on a prisons visit but after much thought I wanted James to meet my new born Ellie, as I knew he wouldn't get to see her for at least 3 years until parole.

On the day of the visit I was nervous taking a tiny baby with us on a long car journey and taking her into a prison. We got into the searching area and to my horror a lady took me and Ellie into a baby changing room where she asked me to remove Ellie's nappy I was mortified, she must have seen this as she told me that it was protocol, I had to remove her nappy and put on one that was pervaded by the prison. Has if that wasn't bad enough I also had to take a drink of Ellie's baby milk or I wasn't allowed to take it in on the visit, we finally got into the visiting hall, we took our seats.

James came in and as soon as he seen Ellie he was over whelmed, he sat for the whole two hours with her, he feed and winded her. For that two hours, it was like for the first time he forgot where he was. The visits became somewhat bonding time for James and Ellie! Ellie is now 6 years old and never seen her uncle on the outside because James cannot prove to a panel of people that don't know him that he's not a risk.

This to me is absolute madness. James has been taken away from a family that love him dearly for 11 years, we will never get over this miscarriage of justice not just for James but to us all!

Knowing James is not coping, self-harming and a few times tried to take his own life breaks my heart. James has been told he has a string of mental health problems which I disagree with has James gets himself mental and physically well to go before parole only to be told his not coming home and he will need to do more courses that his already done and that last 2 years, I believe that would push anyones mental state.

When I speak to James when he's at his lowest he tells me how hard life is in prison and how he just wants to come home, the lack of understanding why the law allows him to go round in circles in the prison system and having no hope is what causes this, I try to reassure him and give him hope but that's hard to do when you have lost hope you're self in the justices system, after these calls I feel helpless, I pray that day we will not get the call that his taking his life. I have now made him promise me that he will keep fighting because we have a family who will not stop until James is reunited with us.

James Mum and Dad states, As James parents not a day goes by that we don't think of our son and the injustice he has faced. The reality of Ipp has kept us for 11 years apart from him for a mattress fire, we serve this sentence this Ipp with James. We feel massive guilt, sadness and anger over Ipp, our son is a good boy it sickens us to think of him in prison 11 year on.

We are getting old now and suffer with ill health, we want our boy home so we can help him build a life for himself and have time with us. Our worse fear is that we will never get to see our son free and happy. We want to say we're massively proud of James for not giving up when times gets hard.

My own observations of this case, out of the all the IPP cases I've looked at, James case has to be the worst and unjust sentence I have come across I do hope the authorities give this case the full attention it deserves and common sense will prevail.

Chapter Nine - Case of Anthony May

On 20th of May Anthony May was arrested and on 13th of July 2005 convicted of Armed Robbery and Possession with Intent to supply a small quantity of drugs. Anthony pleaded guilty at the earliest opportunity and was later sentenced to a 3 year IPP sentence for the robbery and for the drugs offences was sentence to a further 3 years to run concurrently.

What is unique about this case is Anthony had no record of violence before this robbery and was only ever convicted of small amounts of drugs and the courts excepted this was the case however they still felt he was a risk to the public and was their reason for passing such a sentence.

I was of the view like many others that IPP was only to be used against those who have used violence on previous occasions yet Anthony had no history of this.

The reason why Anthony offended in the first place was because he was taking drugs. Dealing with these issues in the first instance should have taken a high priority simply for the fact if Anthony could overcome the drugs he was taking his offending behaviour would stop. Going to the root causes of the crime is the way to stop prisoners offending and makes common sense. This was totally overlooked in this case.

Whilst Anthony deserved a prison sentence and he will be the first to admit that, he didn't warrant the use of IPP. Anthony has been full of remorse for his actions and took full responsibility for them.

Whilst in side Anthony became a model prisoner and immediately wanted to change and address his offending behaviour and throughout his sentence he managed to get off the drugs and clean his act up. He did all the courses he was asked to do and fully complied with his sentence plan.

Anthony took up Computer Studies and achieved an ECDL and completed basic Maths and English. Anthony also got help with past problems things which happened to him when he was young that had affected his life and were very traumatic for him and he managed to get counselling to deal with those matters.

Anthony was doing well in prison and completely turned his life around he also became a prison listener and helped a lot of other inmates. Despite all this good work by Anthony he still went over his tariff set by the trial judge.

In 2008 Anthony instructed a firm of solicitors to represent him at his first oral parole hearing and to give you an insight into what the parole board are looking for before they consider an IPP prisoner for release here is the submissions made on Anthony's behalf.

The first point Anthony's solicitor brings to the parole boards attention is the sentencing remarks of the trial judge that he had pleaded guilty at the earliest opportunity and the court said they were of the opinion that the seriousness of this particular offence is not so serious as to justify the imposition of a sentence of imprisonment for life.

Submissions were made that the Anthony has no history of violent offences, no history of using firearms no history of behaving in this bizarre and highly criminal fashion and bearing in mind his age. The court is able to reach the conclusion that this was not a case which warranted a life sentence.

Further submissions were made that Anthony had done all the courses he was required to do and has remained alcohol and drug free for the duration of his sentence. This was very significant as drugs was the main cause of his offending behaviour.

Pre-sentence report carried out by a probation officer 17/05/05 and on the 24/06/05. Describes the situation which led to Anthony being convicted of Possession with the intent to supply. Anthony was holding 15 ecstasy tablets for a friend who had just left for the pub and would be returning for them in one hour. Anthony was making no financial gain, but the supply' element of his sentence relates to the fact that he would supply the drugs back to his friend. Anthony has never been considered to be a drugs dealer.

Anthony's solicitors asked the parole panel to take into account the agreed guilty plea and that Anthony poses a low risk of harm to the public. His solicitor also pointed out that at an early stage in Anthony's sentence he was very motivated to avoid further offending and this was even prior to conviction. As the parole dossier documents showed Anthony has matured during his 3 years in custody and as such the position of some motivation has got to one of significant motivation. Further submissions were made on Anthony's behalf in relation to the pre-sentence probation officer report which states he was extremely remorseful for his behaviour and what he had put the victim of his crime through. At no point did he try to justify or excused his behaviour on mitigating circumstances such as previous family problems, childhood abuse or an entrenched circle of drug taking associates.

In the pre-sentence report the probation officer quite rightly points out that back then he was a high risk of physiological and emotional harm to the public whilst under the influence of drugs and Alcohol.

Anthony however has addressed all these issues and has consistently throughout his sentence passed the mandatory drug testing on every occasion he has been asked to do one. Minimising any risk of reoffending.

Anthony's Solicitor also pointed out that he had completed all of his sentence plan objectives aimed at reducing any identified risk factors including completing all available courses E.T.S and A.O.L became involved with CARATS, sought counselling and has worked towards improving his education and employability.

Other factors in Anthony's favour was that he had an improved relationship with his step father and his mother sent a letter to the parole board stating he had a loving environment to come home to.

The key issues his solicitor wanted them to consider in the parole hearing was that.

1. He shows victim empathy and does not seek to avoid responsibility.
2. Has consistently met all targets set for him in his sentence plan

3. Has been proactive in seeking out the particular workers and groups that have enabled him to meet his sentence plan.
4. Has made significant progress whilst in custody.
5. Has worked towards his parole and continues to display a high level of motivation to remain offence free.
6. Has had a total of 7 negative MDTS and has been relocated on the drugs free wing.
7. The glowing report on the E.T.S Post Programme.
8. Personal officer report stating that Anthony will not pose a threat to the public on release.

Before this parole hearing Anthony had three setbacks where the date was actually cancelled and he told me how frustrating it was and the stressful it was waiting for a new date. He said imagine being locked up behind a locked door and a green envelope gets slid under your door and every time a let-down a few lines on a white piece of paper and that set the mood for the month.

Anthony had to wait 9 days to be released and even on the release date the licence was wrong and he got out at 1pm but I was free. Apart from probation he said.

Anthony Served 3 years of his sentence before finally being released on licence on 1st June 14th 2008 and has not looked back. Anthony has been out of prison for 7 years and has settled down and got married and now has 3 young children. Anthony is clearly one of the success stories however Anthony does not see it that way and sees himself as a survivor.

"Anthony said I don't know how there can be any success stories of such a devastating sentence. I'm a survivor not a success like someone beating cancer. How can we beat a system that's designed to make you fail at every turn? "

Anthony's now at the stage where he can apply for his probation to be removed as he no longer requires this however when it comes to his licence it stays with him for 99 years and can apply after 10 years to have this removed if he's stayed out of trouble.

Anthony has managed to hold down a steady job and has been out nearly eight years' drug and crime free.

My own personal opinion is Anthony is a remarkable character and has done brilliantly his case shows how difficult it is being a IPP prisoner but he survived it I don't think I could have done it could you?

Chapter Ten Case of Jason Thorne

Jason Thorne was one of the first IPP prisoners to be given this new sentence in 2005 for threats to kill (said in anger and a flippant comment) Most of us have used this phase when we have been angry or upset did doesn't mean we are going to actually do it. Whilst Jason had previous convictions for street fighting (Being one of the boys) he had no other offences of serious violent crime like robbery. Jason was aged 33 when he got this sentence and the trial judge gave him a low tariff of 17 months.

It took Jason 3 to 4 years before he could get on the courses he needed to do, putting him way over his tariff through no fault of his own. Every prison has different courses and Jason should have been sent to those prisons so he could progress through the system.

It transpired that fixed release date prisoners who had to do the same courses were getting preference over IPP prisoners and sometimes the courses were only run twice a year in each prison.

This caused a backlog of IPP prisoners waiting to go on these courses. Furthermore, by the time the next courses were run there was an influx of more fixed term prisoners who were coming into the prison system who needed to do the course further reducing any chance of IPP Prisoners being able to take the courses which they needed to do to show they were a low risk to the parole board.

Jason was refused parole on a few occasions due to the courses not being available for him to do and has been penalised through no fault of his own. They also wanted him to resettle via Prescoed Prison as he had been in jail for so long but many prisoners have been in for 10yrs and been released without attending an open prison first.

Jason is due for Parole in November 2016 and although has now completed the courses this Parole hearing will not take place until January 2017. This is due to the lack of parole board staff and the back log of IPP cases and it appears they are overwhelmed with them.

Interesting point to note is during the courses all IPP prisoners are told to take responsibility for their own actions and quite rightly so however are the parole board going to except responsibility for keeping IPP Prisoners in jail past their tariff date because of their lack of action and or other failings within the system.

Jason at his last parole hearing was denied parole on the sole basis that he hasn't seen his probation officer enough, it was excepted that this was not Jason's fault and that the probation officers was to blame for this for not visiting him. This is an injustice in itself. The bigger question is how many other prisoners have fallen foul of something so trivial like this? Jason should have been released at this parole hearing and even his own offending management officer had recommended he was released and was a low risk to the public.

Jason did get his category D prison status and was sent to Prescoed Open prison but this was hardly any consolation to him when he should have got parole and been released.

In July of 2016 Jason was granted home leave for 2 days however shortly afterwards someone maliciously phoned up the prison making allegations against Jason saying he was bringing drugs back to the prison. Jason was immediately recalled back to prison because of this.

These allegations were investigated by the authorities and not surprisingly they were without foundation. Jason is still in a closed prison but still has his category D status.

Jason went to see his friend Jessica when on day release and it appears now that the authorities have been proven to have acted without just cause by recalling Jason they are now trying to use a condition in his licence which says that he is not to have a relationship with anyone.

Jessica who has been fighting to get Jason out of prison admitted they were together many years ago and that when she saw Jason she realised she had feelings for him (Jason did not know this) however there was no sexual relationship going on.

Jason did feel the same as Jessica (she had no idea he had feelings for her too) Jason and was going to discuss with his Probation officer when he was out on licence if it would be possible to have a relationship with someone. Unfortunately, he was taken back to prison on false allegations and the meeting never took place.

I have seen Jason's Licence conditions and in it states Jason is not allowed to have a relationship with anyone I question whether this is a lawful condition of his licence. Firstly, Article 8 of the Human rights convention states everyone has a right to family life so even if Jason and Jessica wanted to get together they are well within their rights to do so.

Under the Prison Act 1952 section 47 no rules can be made up by the authorities which impinge on a prisoner's civil right. Yet that's exactly what they have done by outlawing Jason having a relationship and putting it in his licence conditions I am of the view this is unlawful. Article 8 goes further and states everyone's entitled to the right of privacy. Where is Jason's and Jessica's right to privacy?

The Prison Authorities know they messed up by recalling Jason for something he did not do and rather than admit they were in the wrong. It appears because it had the clause in his licence that said he was not allowed to have an undisclosed relationship. That they are going to try to use it at his next parole hearing to justify not giving him parole.

The Authorities are trying to use the phone calls between them as evidence of a full-blown relationship i.e. at the end of the conversation they say love you to each other and to be fair even if they were in love it is no business of the authorities. He's not committing any criminal offences and I would like an explanation and so would the public in regards this matter.

Someone who is known to Jason and Jessica have made false malicious allegations against them both and is hell bent on causing as much trouble as they can for them.

Whilst I cannot go into details for legal reasons there is no doubt that someone who knows them both have made false allegations to the prison authorities and to the police.

Whilst all this has been going on The prison authorities seem to have nothing better to do that cause Jason problems over Jessica, saying they had a relationship. They had nothing to disclose to the authorities about their relationship and when Jason went to Jessica's house thought she was married and had moved on.

Jason has now served 11 years that makes him 9 years plus over his tariff how can you justify such a sentence and then try to keep him in prison longer because he likes a woman and if he was allowed to would have a proper stable relationship with her. He has not breeched anyone trust and has done nothing wrong. I am of the view he should have been released years ago.

One thing Jason's case does is open your eyes to is the petty things which you can end up back in prison for the most trivial of things. In Jason's case all it took was someone to make a false allegation and they took him back into prison without any evidence he had done something wrong, what ever happened to innocent until proved guilty?

At a whim of a disgruntled person anyone can say what they like about an IPP prisoner and they will be locked up again for no good reason. How can the system justify that and how are they going to deal with injustices like Jason's in the future?

I hope common sense will prevail at Jason's next parole hearing and hope he is given a chance to rebuild his life.

All cases were provided by Katherine Gleeson who has campaigned tirelessly on IPP Sentences. Katherine has first-hand experience in that one of her relatives served a IPP Sentence and successfully got them out of prison. At one stage Katherine got a massive petition of over 27000 signatures to abolish the IPP Sentence and she is still fighting for others left behind.

Here is a short List of useful cases on IPP where the Courts have overturned IPP sentences and substituted them for a determinate sentence

Kyri Argyropoulos successfully appeals IPP sentence for axe-wielding petrol station robber.

Kyri Argyropoulos represented MS who had pleaded guilty to robbery and possession of an axe which he brandished after jumping on the counter of a petrol station less than 2 weeks after his release from prison. Although MS had 3 previous convictions for robbery, and also for possession of an imitation firearm, his IPP sentence was quashed on appeal and a determinate one of 3 years substituted.

IPP sentence quashed

12/02/2010

Mr Sutherland was convicted and sentenced at Lincoln Crown Court in October 2006 in respect of sexual offences. He was sentenced to a 9-month tariff under Section 225 of the Criminal Justice Act 2003.

On 5 February 2010 the Court agreed and substituted an 18-month determinate sentence.

The appellant was sentenced in 2006 to imprisonment for public protection (IPP) with a tariff of nine months (less time spent on remand) for sexual offences. He appealed against sentence with leave of the Single Judge.

In the leading case of *Lang* [2006] 2 Cr App R (S) 3 the Court of Appeal emphasised that before an IPP sentence could be imposed sentencers had to be satisfied that there was a significant risk of the offender committing further specified offences and that he/she would cause serious harm as a result. Serious harm is defined as death or serious personal injury, whether physical or psychological.

It was argued on the appellant's behalf that there was no evidence that the victims were caused serious harm as a result of the index offences. Neither was there any evidence that the appellant had caused serious harm through previous offending. Whilst the absence of serious harm at the time of sentence was not determinative it was a highly relevant factor for the judge to consider in determining whether there was a significant risk of serious harm in the future. In all the circumstances it was submitted that the sentencing judge had failed to conduct a proper assessment of the appellant's risk of causing serious harm through the commission of further specified offences and that it had been wrong in principle to impose a sentence of IPP.

The Court of Appeal agreed and quashed the sentence of IPP, substituting a determinate sentence of 18 months' imprisonment. The Court also varied the terms of a sexual offences prevention order to ensure that the terms were no wider than was necessary for the protection of the public and were drafted sufficiently precisely that the appellant and anyone charged with enforcing the SOPO would know what he must and must not do in order to comply

The appellant was sentenced under the dangerous offender regime as originally enacted, and therefore if the judge concluded that the appellant was dangerous he was required to impose a sentence of IPP. The regime was amended with effect from 14th July 2008 by the Criminal Justice and Immigration Act 2008.

As will be obvious from the above this appeal was lodged over 2 years out of time, the grounds having come too light when the appellants case was reviewed in preparation for the parole process. His success shows that prison law practitioners should be alert to the possibility of bringing out of time appeals in appropriate cases. The case also illustrates the importance of ensuring that prohibitions in a sexual offences prevention order are drafted with care and precision to ensure that they are readily understood and go no further than is necessary in order to protect the public from sexual harm

10/04/2006
In the case of R v Baird (and another) [2006] EWCA Crim 993, on 7th April 2006 the Court of Appeal Criminal Division quashed the sentence of imprisonment for public protection and imposed a determinate sentence. This decision re-affirms and emphasises the points made in *Lang* in relation to "dangerous offenders".

R v. David BAIRD (and another) [2006] EWCA Crim 993

On the 24th October 2005, at the Manchester Crown Court, the defendant was sentenced to imprisonment for public protection, pursuant to section 225 of the Criminal Justice Act 2003, by HHJ Hammond for two offences of robbery and seven offences of theft. The minimum period to be served was specified as three years for the robberies and 18 months for the thefts, to be served concurrently.

The facts of the offences were that over a three-week period the defendant, usually accompanied by another, had on nine occasions entered small shops in the Manchester area. Under the guise of purchasing items or waiting to be served he had then either snatched the cash register or snatched money from the register. In two of the offences some force had been used hence the charges of robbery. No weapon had been used or threatened and the defendant was unmasked during all offences. The pleas were all well in advance of the trial date.

As the offences all post-dated the commencement of the "dangerous offender" provisions in the Criminal Justice Act 2003 it was necessary for an assessment of dangerousness to be carried out by the sentencing judge. HHJ Hammond indicated to counsel that he was assuming the defendant was dangerous pursuant to section 229(3) of the CJA, as his antecedents showed a previous specified offence. The defendant had only one previous specified offence - a conviction for ABH from June 2004. The learned judge asked for submissions why it was unreasonable to apply the assumption of dangerousness.

The sentencing exercise predated the Court of Appeal decision of **R v. Lang and Others (2005) EWCA Crim 2864**. Nevertheless, submissions where made that the current offences revealed no evidence of serious physical harm. The most violence that was used was during the two robberies where the staff were pushed or bumped into and one cashier's lip was caught by the defendant's arm. There was also no evidence of any psychological harm to any of the victims.

The learned judge found that there was no reason not to apply the assumption. He stated that it was obvious that the nature of the offences meant that psychological harm was likely to have been caused to the shop staff and for this reason there was no reason not to apply the assumption that there was a significant risk that the defendant would cause serious harm to the public in the future.

On the 7th April 2006, the Court of Appeal Criminal Division quashed the sentence of imprisonment for public protection and imposed a determinate sentence. Rather than simply doubling up the minimum term, it agreed with submissions that the minimum term was too long and imposed a determinate term of five years' imprisonment.

In coming to this conclusion, the Court of Appeal firstly reminded itself of paragraph 17(iii) of Lang that, "If the foreseen specified offence is serious, there will clearly be some cases, though not by any means all, in which there may be a significant risk of serious harm. For example, robbery is a serious offence. But it can be committed in a wide variety of ways many of which do not give rise to a significant risk of serious harm. Sentencers must therefore guard against assuming there is a significant risk of serious harm merely because the foreseen specified offence is serious".

The Court then went on to state as follows:
"In the case of the appellant Baird it is argued that these offences involved no weapons, that they principally relied on the element of surprise, and that minimal force only was resorted to when surprise was not effective on its own. There were no threats and there was no evidence of serious harm in the sense defined by section 224(3) of the 2003 Act.

Nearly all his previous offending was acquisitive crime. The pre-sentence report did not suggest that the future foreseen harm was serious. This means, it is argued, that the judge fell into error, the error being to assume that the kind of distress suffered by the victims in this case was sufficient to qualify as serious harm if it occurred again in the future, and it fell foul of the assumption warned against in the passage we have quoted in Lang and Others.

It is also the case that the matters that the sentencer should take into account, as set out in paragraph 17(ii) of that decision, are not addressed by the judge because he did not have the evidence to do so. In paragraph 47 in Lang and Others that principle is set out in one of the appeals. The court said:

"Although the author of the pre-sentence report was right to say that there is always a risk of psychological harm in robbery, it is not necessarily either a significant risk or a risk of serious harm; as we have earlier indicated the degree of both risk and harm must be evidenced. Furthermore, rapid repetition of offences in itself does not, as the Recorder suggested, demonstrate a significant risk of serious harm....

We agree with the submission made that the guidance given by Lang, had it been available to the judge, would have resulted in this sentence not being passed. These are indeterminate sentences, tantamount in all but one respect to life sentences, and should only be passed on low-level offending such as this if all the requirements set out in Lang are met. They were not in this case."

This decision therefore re-affirms and emphasises the points made in Lang. In particular, the explicit statement that IPP sentences are for all intents and purposes life-sentences and should not therefore be passed on low-level offending, even where the offences carry the name of "robbery", unless a number of requirements are met, is a timely and important reminder to sentencing judges.

Successful appeal of IPP sentence

On 21 June 2007 our client, T, received an IPP sentence with a minimum term of 3 ½ years minus time spent on remand. This was for an offence of wounding with intent to inflict GBH.

The Court of Appeal accepted that while there may have been a significant risk of T committing further offences, there was not sufficient evidence to demonstrate that the commission of further offences would pose a significant risk of serious harm being caused, a crucial requirement of an IPP sentence. T's other offences were for low level nonviolent and non-sexual offences. The section 18 wounding could therefore be seen as being out of character.

T only had one previous specified offence which was an attempted robbery from June 1996. He was convicted of the index offence some 11 years later, a significant gap. The index offence and this previous specified offence were completely unconnected in type.

Furthermore, the Judge had not applied sentencing in the manner set out in the case of Lang but had gone straight from the fact of a previous conviction to the finding of dangerousness without looking at the detail of the previous offence.

The Court of Appeal quashed T's IPP sentence and replaced it with a determinate sentence of 7 years.

This is a fantastic result for T. He has been released on license and has less than 12 months until his Sentence Expiry Date. Despite being two years over tariff T had struggled to make progress through the prison system and had remained in closed conditions unable to make headway before the Parole Board. This is now behind him as he now out on license in the community. (Swain and Co Solicitors)

In a Recent case, however The Court of Appeal said that it is up to parliament to sort out the mess IPP sentences has left since the government abolished this sentence leaving it much harder to bring judicial review proceedings.

Many of those campaigning too free their loved ones believe when they abolished IPP it should have been retrospective and due to the fact many IPP prisoners are over their tariff should have been released on time served. To be honest it would be very difficult to argue against that when you look at some of the petty crimes some of these IPP prisoners were sentenced for.

I hope the Government will look at all the cases of IPP sympathetically and although there has been whispers of all IPP prisoner's being released by 2017 actions speak louder than words.

Chapter Twelve Conclusions

One thing which really strikes me from my point of view in relation to IPP Sentences is that they were used on the youngsters between the ages of 17 to 22 and that many of those sentenced to this unjust sentence could have been dealt with a normal determinate prison sentence.

IPP sentences were supposed to have been used on the most repeat violent offenders however too many prisoners were given IPP for the most trivial things like stealing a mobile phone. How do the criminal Justice system justify giving out sentences like this whilst serious violent offenders get a fixed prison term?

Whilst I'm sure the government had good intentions when bringing out IPP sentences it has to be said the interpretation of the Act has caught many trivial offenders rather than the seriously violent criminals it was supposed to have applied to causing massive injustices to many prisoners and their families.

It also has to be said too what about the real victims of the crimes when they see violent offenders getting light sentences which others in effect get a life sentence through IPP for mobile phone robbery and motoring offences. This cannot be right and in my view, is a breach of natural Justice.

Some of the cases, and people I've interviewed for this book recognise that their loved one deserved a prison sentence and do have sympathy for the victim's family however it is important that the sentence which is given out by the courts is a fair and just sentence to those who committed the crimes. IPP has been a stain on our criminal justice system and was rightly abolished. What needs to be done now in the interests of justice is to get all the less serious cases IPP prisoners out of the prison system as soon as possible.

They will of course will all need specialist help when they come out which needs to be provided upon release. Many will suffer from mental health conditions such as post-traumatic stress disorder and will find it difficult to adjust to normal life without the necessary help.

Many IPP Prisoners have done all the courses asked of them and many have reports showing that the risk of reoffending is very low so there is no reason for them to be still in prison when with the right help can be released back into society and who can make a significant contribution to it.

The courses which the IPP prisoners needs to do should be available in every prison and there are long waiting lists for those on IPP to do these courses. For one course, it can take up to eight months to get on it yet every IPP prisoner has to do nine courses before he can go to the parole board with any chance of getting out.

This cannot be right and more funding needs to be forthcoming so that the IPP prisoners can get these courses all done so they are ready for release. If the courses are not available how can the IPP Prisoner be held responsible for not doing them when he or she comes before the parole board?

Injustice comes in many shapes and forms and those injustices are not always as clear cut as a miscarriage of justice cases are, never the less Ipp sentences were indeed an injustice and they were not fit for its intended purpose that's why IPP was abolished in 2012. I hope the government will be brave enough to right those wrongs.

I hope this book will bring to the government attention the injustice of those left behind on IPP and do hope Members of Parliament will raise the cases highlighted and that the House of Lords will lend weight to my arguments that most IPP prisoners have to be released.

Acknowledgements

I would like to thank the families who have shared their stories with me and the contributions from those on IPP sentences it has really opened my eyes to the unjust sentences many have been given, I would like to thank Shirley Lloyd and Kathrine Gleeson who have championed the cause of IPP prisoners, and have been an inspiration for me to write this book two amazing people.

I would like to thank The Howard League for Penal Reform, The Prison Reform Trust for their reports into IPP prisoners two amazing organisation who have helped prisoners tremendously for many years.

I would also like to thank Karen Cooper at the Centre for Criminology University of Oxford for her report into IPP Prisoners which has made a huge difference. Keep up the good work.

A big thank you goes out to Radio 4's Zoe Conway who did a brilliant article of one of the cases in this book and brought the injustice to my attention. Thank you.

I would like to thank Mathew Stansbury QC of Garden Court North Chambers for all the work he has done to help IPP prisoners, some featured in this book. Amazing work.

I would also like to thank two vice news Journalists Maeve Mccleagan and Ben Bryant who are based in London for their reports into IPP prisoners both have done amazing work and highlighted the injustice of many prisoners. Thank you.

I would also like to thank Ex HM inspectorate of Prisons Ann Owers and HM inspectorate of Probation Service for their in depth joint report on the problems of IPP. Thank you.

I'd like to say a big thank you too Inside Time the Prison newspaper who have worked tirelessly to highlight the injustices of IPP. A big thank you to them for highlighting the Parole deal written by Dr Michael Naughton of Bristol University.

Thank you to B Stanford of Wymott Prison your contribution has helped tremendously.

Would also like to that Martin Shipton for bringing to my attention the new figures released on IPP Prisoners and the Ministry of Justice for providing them.

I would also like to acknowledge the families who lost loved ones to this IPP sentence in total 16 prisoners died my thoughts are with you all and your families, god bless.

Michael O'Brien 2016

Printed in Great
Britain
by Amazon